BEGINNING RIGHTLY

Beginning
RIGHTLY

DANIEL JENSEN

The Bookmark
Santa Clarita, California

Jensen, Daniel L., 1927-
    Beginning rightly : a collection of five talks / by
Daniel L. Jensen.
    p. cm.
    LCCN 2005928141
    ISBN-13: 978-0-930227-77-7
    ISBN-10: 0-930227-77-8

    1. Christian Science. 2. Spiritual healing.
3. Consciousness--Religious aspects--Christianity.
4. Metaphysics.   I. Title.

BX6945.J46 2005   289.5
                             QBI05-600076

Published by
The Bookmark
Post Office Box 801143
Santa Clarita, California 91380

CONTENTS

FOREWORD

This is a collection of talks given by Daniel Jensen when he was invited to speak at meetings held for experienced Christian Scientists. They are more advanced than a Christian Science lecture, and yet not so long or deep as a teacher's address for the members of an association. Thus they fill a unique niche in the published works of the past. The talks are "reader-friendly" for each one is as though Mr. Jensen were explaining to you personally how to make a better demonstration of Christian Science.

Often the focus of his talk is on overcoming age. He discusses the need to do prayerful work regarding the laws of heredity, the belief in ancestry, the celebration of birthdays, and the acceptance of age as inevitable. He shows how important it is to realize that we are immortal now.

As an experienced practitioner and teacher, he gives many outstanding examples of his own healing work to illustrate how effective prayer in Christian Science can be. He explains how to deal with many day-to-day challenges, but he is especially strong on the need to handle the mortal beliefs of time, age, birth, and death that are often the underlying causes of chronic illness. We must not delay the handling of the subtle claims of age if we expect to be free of them in our advancing years. This warning is accompanied by the spiritual enlightenment needed to help us make this vital demonstration.

BEGINNING RIGHTLY

In *Science and Health with Key to the Scriptures,* Mary Baker Eddy tells us, "To begin rightly is to end rightly." This is what I'd like to share with you — "beginning rightly." In our prayers and in our treatments, from which premise do we begin? — Spirit, or matter?

Mortal mind presents its material claims of disease, discord and lack to all mankind, it seems. And since most of the world is ignorantly deceived into accepting these material sense pictures as instant reality, they undertake to heal them in the only way they know — materially. However, almost the first thing a student of Christian Science learns is that we do not, in the practice of Christian Science, use material means for healing. Gradually, we come to understand something of why we do not, and how we turn to spiritual means alone. This premise in the solution is pretty generally accepted among Scientists. Most Scientists believe in using metaphysics, and using it alone — not to mix it. There is one vitally important area where all too often we go astray. Any experienced Christian Science practitioner will tell you that nine out of ten patients come wanting metaphysical help, but to do what? To heal a material body, a material situation — through spiritual means.

What does this effort reveal? Well, it tells us unmistakably that we, too, have been deceived by the "primary error" — the reality of matter. We have been duped into accepting the wrong premise — that matter is real, that man is mortal, and that it is matter that needs healing. This, of course, is not beginning rightly. True, we are not using material means to solve our problem, but the problem itself is seen to be a material one. Our view of the problem is often as material as the doctors' of disease, or the referees' in bankruptcy. The only difference in our methods is that we attempt

1

to use spiritual means to cure it. Is this Christian Science? No, I'm afraid not. It would probably be classified as a form of "mind over matter," or psychosomatic medicine, Christian Science style, or at best, faith healing.

In *Science and Health* Mrs. Eddy admonishes, "It is mental quackery to make disease a reality — to hold it as something seen and felt — and then to attempt its cure through Mind." Now nothing could say it any clearer than that, but isn't that what we often find ourselves doing?

In our discussion of beginning rightly, let's consider an actual case. I received a call one afternoon from a man who despairingly told me that the finest clinics in the state had agreed that his mother would be dead of a malignancy within two weeks. They said it had spread over her entire body, and there was nothing that could be done. So they were turning to Christian Science as a last hope! He then volunteered a detailed description of the medical diagnosis and evidence. As you can see, mortal mind, the playwright, was carefully setting the scene.

I agreed to visit the patient. When I arrived, one element of sense testimony after another was convincingly presented by the medical nurses in attendance. No medicine or treatment was being given because they said there wasn't anything that could be done. It appeared that every argument mortal mind could devise was set forth. A picture of incurability and hopelessness was depicted.

Now, consider that you are the practitioner presented with such a picture. You are, perhaps, at the most crucial point in that case. For it is here that the most basic decision must be made, and it must be made correctly in order to facilitate a healing. In spite of the vividness of the sense testimony and its claim to reality, there is a choice to be made.

When I was in college, I had a professor who every morning when we came in, would say, "Mere repetition does not insure learning." It's the only thing in the course I remember. So, you may observe some repetition here.

Now, how will you view the problem? Which premise will you accept? Will you accept the first premise — that matter, the body, is real; that it has substance, life, sensation, yet is destructible in nature; that it must be repaired or restored, one way or another, physically or metaphysically? It's the body that you find yourself looking at. And when it hurts, it makes it more real. Or will you accept the second premise — that Spirit is real and that man is totally spiritual, eternal, perfect, and indestructible; that this so-called matter is but a mental picture — a mental picture that is unreal and illusory. Which premise is to be accepted at the outset in your work?

Here in the calm of a hypothetical situation, the choice of a spiritual premise is pretty obvious, isn't it? But as we all know, we can often be partially or completely deceived by mortal mind's mental picture before we know it, and find ourselves accepting the material premise.

When I went into the Christian Science practice, my teacher illustrated unforgettably this point of choosing the correct premise. Early in her practice, her infant son had become paralyzed from the waist down with a belief of polio. You can imagine how earnestly that mother worked — hours everyday. And then, naturally enough humanly, she would look under the blanket to see if he could move his little legs when she finished the treatment. This went on for four solid months, and finally she went to a practitioner herself. She told the circumstances to the practitioner, who just smiled, and made one simple revealing statement: "Quit peeking, dear." And she saw immediately what she had been doing.

She went home and gave that child a treatment as she should have to begin with. The next morning when she went to bathe the child, he about jumped out of the pan! No atrophy, no time of recovery! In telling this to me, she said, "It never occurred to me to look at his legs again. What had that to do with it? Nothing. *Nothing*."

I sometimes do this when I'm working on something and the evidence appears pretty real. I just say to myself, "Nothing.

Nothing," to emphasize it, because that is exactly what we are dealing with — a mental illusion.

Even the most experienced Scientists can be deceived, it seems. One of Mrs. Eddy's students told of an incident when our Leader suddenly turned from the bedside of a critically ill patient she was treating. She walked to the window, and in abject humility, quietly exclaimed, "My dear heavenly Father, please forgive me for looking at matter." The healing followed immediately. There was simply a change in premise, leaving the deception of matter for the spiritual reality.

When mortal mind gradually or abruptly presents its vivid mental images to human consciousness, its picture of disease, discord, lack, it always appears to be a material condition or situation, just as it does in our night dreams. We must be and remain alert to the fact that its picture is a mental deception, a lie, not reality, as Mrs. Eddy's experience shows.

May I dwell on this for a moment, because it is such an important point? Mrs. Eddy realized how deceptive sense testimony can be — particularly when it hurts. She said that sleep and mesmerism explain the mythical nature of material sense. What is a myth? It's a make-believe story, it's an illusion, isn't it? Why would she choose those two things to explain what we were experiencing? Because it appears very real. Everyone has experienced dreams, and how real they seem, or we wouldn't cry out or laugh or moan in a sleeping dream. But we know immediately upon waking that it was a total illusion. If you were driving a ten-ton locomotive and you woke up, what happened to that ten tons of steel when you woke up?

In regard to her use of sleep or the dream, you might find it interesting to go to the third series of *We Knew Mary Baker Eddy*, (page 44). She wrote a letter to Calvin Hill, who was suffering from a problem of a lung disease. Now he had not told her, but she discerned this. He was terrified because his father had passed on from tuberculosis. She told him that this is no more real in your waking dream than it is in your sleeping dream. She told him to go to page 188 of *Science and Health*, which talks about the waking and sleeping dreams. To supplement this, may I recommend that you go to page 250 of the textbook which includes this question: "Now I ask, Is there any more reality in the waking dream of mortal existence that in the sleeping dream? There cannot be. . . " You see, she was trying to get across the idea by comparing it with the dream, because it is a very apt comparison, and helps us realize that what we are seeing now is a dream.

Today hardly anyone, particularly among the young, has ever seen anyone hypnotized. But in her day, hypnotists were a part of almost every vaudeville act. Everyone on the street knew what hypnotism was and most of them had seen it — that is why she used the example of mesmerism. At first I saw this more clearly through hypnotic suggestion, because I've seen a lot of people hypnotized. But the dream is spoken about again and again in her writings, because it illustrates the two are similar. They are almost identical. Once we realize this, it changes the whole nature of your thinking if you can bring that to bear on it.

Now, I'll just tell you one little experience. My dad, when he was a young man, was rooming with another young man. They went to a show one night and there was a hypnotist there. My dad's roommate volunteered to go up on the stage. He was hypnotized and told that he was sitting on a hot cook stove. He was actually sitting on a little bench. But he was squirming and squirming, and pretty soon he's in agony, to the delight of the audience, because they could see there was not anything going on. He was screaming and yelling in pain, and finally they let him off. My dad said when they got home, he had big water blisters all over his body, so real had been the mental image. And we see this all the time in Christian Science practice — hypnotic suggestion.

Mrs. Eddy used a very apt means of explaining to us the unreality of it. She says this is the primary error — the claim of reality in matter. She warns us, "Admit the existence of matter, and you admit that mortality (and therefore disease) has a foundation in fact." (*Science and Health*), and elsewhere, "Matter is . . . sometimes beautiful, always erroneous." (ibid)

A woman once came to Edward Kimball complaining that she had yellow canary feathers growing all over her arms. He said, "Madam, there are no canary feathers on your arms." But she was just adamant about this, saying, "Of course there are. Look at this." Canary feathers were as real to her as anything else. Now, how much time do you think Mr. Kimball spent trying to get rid of feathers? His task, he knew, was simply to dissolve a mental illusion — a delusion. He did this by acknowledging the spiritual fact that man is the image and likeness of God and therefore perfect now! In such a case, it is comparatively easy to avoid trying to change matter and to start from a spiritual premise, because we know that women do not grow feathers — birds grow feathers.

But what if the woman had presented arms that were covered with an ugly-appearing skin disease? Wouldn't it be tempting to start from a material premise and try to heal matter? In reality, however, would the situation be one bit more material? Wouldn't it, too, be just a mental illusion? Wouldn't the same spiritual premise be the correct starting point? Of course it would. But it requires consistent alertness to be instantly aware that matter, good or bad appearing, is the illusion, and not to be tempted to assume the premise of material reality, and then try to heal it.

Another very helpful assistance in learning to begin rightly is that wonderful short paragraph on page 123 of our textbook. It reads, "The verity of Mind shows conclusively how it is that matter seems to be, but is not. Divine Science, rising above physical theories, excludes matter, resolves things into thoughts, and replaces the objects of material sense with spiritual ideas."

Now, let us look a little more closely at the reminders contained in this statement. You see, we can't take these beautiful things that she says just on their face value. We've got to think about them a little. As an example of this, I would like to refer you to the first testimony in *The Christian Science Journal*, March 1918. [See page 85 for this testimony.] You will find it probably the most remarkable testimony you have ever read. But the thing is, when you hear of someone being able to hear for the first time in her life after twenty minutes of reading *Science and Health*, and she's hearing with an ear where the eardrum and ear bone had been surgically removed — hearing the tick of a tiny little watch, besides the other things that she was healed of — you begin to think it might be worthwhile.

I'm referring this to you because of the manner in which she read. There are two or three paragraphs that describe how she read, and it is so important to see how she went about reading. That is why I'm talking about these statements on page 123, of taking them apart and thinking about them. Now, in the statement, "the verity of Mind" (Truth) shows us "conclusively" — that is, beyond question, decisively, absolutely, categorically — that matter only "seems to be, but is not." It is "divine Science" which enables us to rise "above physical theories," to "exclude matter," and to "resolve things into thoughts" — that is, to see that everything which appears to be material is only thought, a mental concept. Are you occupying a matter body, or is the body in you? When we see this, of course, the claim is recognized as a mental one, and can be dealt with. But so long as one is dealing with "things," with matter, he's not even in the ball game. He's still out in the parking lot.

Why is this resolution of things into thoughts so important? Well, in the first place, when you are dealing with thoughts, you're dealing with something that can be changed, replaced, corrected. Who ever heard of an unchangeable thought? Do you see what this does to the claim of incurability? Who ever heard of an incurable thought? There has never been such a thing. This resolution of things into thoughts allows us to see things as simply illusions, mental mistakes or errors, rather than as realities or frightful material conditions.

Mrs. Eddy required members of her household, if they had

a claim, to put two words before it, "belief of." If they had a stomach ache, it was "belief of a stomach ache." What does that do the minute you put "belief of" in front of it? You have a different ball game. It's hard to think of it as matter, if you do that simple thing. Therefore it keeps us from trying to heal, repair, or restore materially. We now recognize it to be mental illusion.

Have you ever thought of trying to heal the train tracks that look to you and to everyone else as though they came together just outside of town? And why not? Because you have come to know, through experience or education, that their merging is an illusion. Imagine trying to get your practitioner to heal the merging tracks. It would be a little embarrassing, wouldn't it? The need would be to realize that they never merged in the first place. We simply don't try to heal feathers, or merging tracks, or anything that we understand to be a mental illusion. If we understand it to be a mental illusion, it would be silly to try to fix it. The challenge, therefore, is to look through the false testimony of the senses, the material picture presented, and recognize and understand it to be a mental error.

And how do you do this? You know the answer so well. *Dwell on the spiritual fact as taught in Divine Science.* Dwell on it so single-mindedly and resolutely that only this truth has reality to you. The illusion will become self-evident. This is destroying the illusion through divine metaphysics, and not through an act of will power. It is the power of Truth that heals. You see, all that has happened is that this false belief has settled in human consciousness, and it has become temporarily a reality to us. That's why we think we see the flu, or a broken arm, or lack, or disease. It is that false belief which has to be dealt with. The healing process of this is set out in the Science of the Christ.

Let me go very briefly into that process, because sometimes we just get so absolute in our approach to things that we forget the basics of it. First, we are going to deny. Our denial doesn't have to be a complicated thing. Bicknell Young set it up so simply.

He said, "First you realize that there is no origin to that belief. Second, that it has no substance, no reality in its lying plane. Third, that it has no law to support it. No source, no substance, no law." No source, no substance, no law.

What you are doing with that denial is simply wiping the mental blackboard clean. There is very little healing going on about this denial, but the denial is an important part of the Science of the Christ. I'm just reviewing some of the simplest things Mrs. Eddy tells us in our textbook about it.

And then we go to affirmation. We affirm the spiritual facts. Now, why do we do this? Because it's the spiritual fact that destroys the lie. Nothing else can or will. You wipe the blackboard clean, and then you affirm these truths about man. This is the active ingredient. In *Science and Health* Mrs. Eddy says, "Truth has a healing effect, even when not fully understood." That's always very helpful to me. Sometimes it takes us a while to get these truths. We work on them, and we turn them every which way. That's why I mentioned this testimony, because the woman turned it every which way, looking at it. Her eyes were so weak she couldn't read but one line at a time. And she did not even think of being healed. She wasn't declaring these truths to fix anything. She was doing it simply to see the truth in them. And that's what we are doing. We are just seeing the truth, the Christ-truth, because that is what has the power which destroys the lie that appears so real to us. This is part of beginning rightly.

As this goes on, this truth without a conscious effort, is quietly destroying the lie. You know yourself that sometimes in working and knowing the truth about something, you've had claims healed that you were not even working on. I've often had that with patients. When you realize that it is the power of the truth, then it takes away your personal responsibility. You declare the truth — it enforces itself. That's where the power lies.

For a moment, let's focus a bit more specifically on the particular challenge of supply. When I have served on boards of various philanthropic organizations, our chief concerns were with raising money and then deciding who should receive it. We usually had some criteria for selecting the recipients, as well as a few professional fund-raisers in our midst who were willing to give us pointers on how to contact prospective donors, and which buttons to press. Everything about our efforts was built on a humanly good motive or purpose, but utilized material methods. Inevitably, material methods bring with them their material beliefs of deficiency, scarcity, shortage, fear and lack.

No wonder our Leader advises against the use of such methods. In *Retrospection and Introspection* she says, "Christian Science shuns whatever involves material means for the promotion of spiritual ends." At one time she commended an article by Mr. Farlow in *The American Business Man*, which said, among other things: "Sometimes individual prosperity is not rightly grounded, and like a house with inadequate foundation, it must therefore be taken down and rebuilt . . . . That which is not rightly done is a misdoing, not a real accomplishment, and painful as the ordeal may seem to the one concerned, the sooner there is an undoing and a re-doing, the better. What appears to be loss under circumstances is not loss but gain. If our riches are not fittingly acquired, they are not really ours, and the sooner we lose them and learn our actual situation, the better."

Isn't it wonderful that you can be a part of an effort that is based on a spiritual concept of supply? You are building on the Rock! This uplifted premise allows you, as you put your unselfish purpose of giving and sharing into action, to grow spiritually, and to help others grow as well. Isn't this spiritual growth our individual "life purpose"? our very reason for being? the spiritual growth you're making?

We are not striving to be the richest man in the graveyard, you know, but to progress spiritually in what Mrs. Eddy calls "earth's preparatory school." We are all in school. Problems that come to us look so bad. We ask, "Why does this have to happen to me?

10

I went to Sunday School every week, and I did all the right things, and why did this have to happen?"

It's part of the learning process — learning problems that are coming to us. It's the way you learn algebra, or anything else. You're taught a lot of theories, and then they send home problems that night for you to work out. That's how you learn it. You didn't learn it by just reading the theories. It's in solving the problems that it becomes ours to use instinctively and quickly and automatically when these things are presented to us.

Is the belief of lack basically any different from the other faces that mortal mind wears — disease, sin, turmoil, strife? I'm talking about this right now because that is what you are going to be facing, basically. You simply can't stand aghast at a belief of lack. Are the rules any different? Do we start out to heal feathers, the delusion? Don't we have to "begin rightly" in order to "end rightly" with this error, as with any other error? Our Leader provides us with a clear sense of supply when she says, "God gives you His spiritual ideas, and in turn, they give you daily supplies. Never ask for tomorrow; it is enough that divine Love is an ever-present help; and if you wait, never doubting, you will have all you need every moment." (*Miscellaneous Writings*)

Isn't that beautifully simple and direct? Spiritual ideas, she says, are what God provides. Now, starting with this realization that there is an absolutely unlimited supply of divine ideas and that the activity of an idea can never be impaired or depleted, we begin to see that we are dealing with infinity itself! Why? Because supply is as unlimited and ever-present as the supreme Giver.

Mortal mind tries, through its delusion of finiteness, to mesmerize man into accepting that he has somehow been separated from God's inexhaustible flow of ideas — his birthright. This sense, this beclouding belief of separation, causes him to feel incapable of accepting or seeing these supply-producing ideas — ideas supported and enforced by divine law. It's like the miser who starves to death right outside the bank where he has millions unknown to him.

It is the elimination of this befogging belief that we are concerned with, isn't it? We are not trying to create more supply, but are interested in having revealed what is already provided by our infinite source, and what alone can remove this murky cloud, leaving revealed spiritual provision? What allowed Hagar to see the well and to find help for her child? It was God's angel, His spiritual idea or Christ. And that's what allows us to see the same.

I know this works. I'm going to transgress and tell a personal experience that illustrates this point. It did to me, beautifully. When I got out of the Navy, I went to law school at the University of California. After the second year, a friend of mine who was in the third year, was about to take the bar exam. He said, "Why don't you take the bar with me?" I said, "Ha-ha-ha. The third year is the hardest year of law school, with thousands of cases to be read, and the heaviest courses." He said, "Come on, you can do that." Well, I went in and talked to the dean at this big law school, and he just laughed at me. He said, "Why nobody's ever done that — you can't do that! You can't pass the bar with two years."

I left his office and went downtown and talked to my mother's Christian Science teacher. He said the most wonderful thing to me. He said, "When you are going to school, all you are doing is pulling aside the curtains of limitation to leave revealed what is already there." To leave revealed! I learned the third year in two weeks. I took all the tests and got straight A's. I took the bar and passed it. It was the first time it had ever been done in the history of the University of California. Not because I was bright. There were a lot of fellows in the class who were brighter. But I got a glimpse of the source. Just a glimpse. But it was enough. That's what we are doing — getting a glimpse of the infinity of supply.

God's laws are perfectly reciprocal. There are laws of being which coordinate and are fitly joined together. What is apparent in human thought as one person or thing supplying the need of another person or thing is actually the reciprocal law of being reflecting the wholeness of itself. We should more and more recognize and utilize this reciprocal law of being which is ever in operation on our behalf, and of those with whom we deal.

It is sometimes said that we do our work in the absolute, the spiritual, and it manifests itself in the world of symbols — humanly. One thing we do know is, we don't start out to heal lack, or feathers, or disease, or any other illusion or delusion metaphysically. We practice the Science of the Christ by denying and understanding the falsity of the belief, and affirming with confidence and constancy the Christ-truth of man's continuing relationship to God. This truth dissolves the misleading lie of mortal mind. It's all that can or does destroy this false belief, and leave revealed man's unbroken unity with God. Nothing else can or will. We call this healing, but its results are simply the side-effects of the affirmation of what is real!

In short, lack isn't truly overcome by getting more money, education, or possessions, but by relinquishing the belief of limitation. Supply isn't found by accumulating, but in eliminating the beclouding belief of lack. And that is all you are doing. In that temporary help you give, it sometimes helps to give a little lift when patients have been working, and working, and working, and they just seem to be exhausted. Sometimes I tell them, "You go home and go to sleep. I'll take it here for a while." And just the thought that this burden is going off them for a little bit enables them to break the burden of that disease — dis-ease. And sometimes that is what you are doing. You're breaking something of the spell, and allowing them to get a glimpse of the fact that truth is quietly at work all of the time destroying the lie. Real supply is not found in things coming to us. Rather it is discovered in ideas which appear through us — through the transparency, clarity, purity, and spirituality of enlightened thought.

Mrs. Eddy tells us, "Matter examined in the light of divine metaphysics disappears." (*Science and Health*) Of course it does. She says it again and again. When she wrote the "Scientific State-

13

ment of Being," the first time she wrote it as, "There is no matter; all is infinite Mind and its infinite manifestation." Then to make it more palatable, she changed it to the way it is now. But if you take the first sentence the way it is now, there is still no matter.

In *Miscellany* she says, *"Spirit is all,"* and she says that in italics. When she says something in italics, you'd better look. Then she says, "There is no matter is not only the axiom of true Christian Science, but it is the only basis upon which this Science can be demonstrated." Now, if anybody says anything cold turkey, that's it. There's no messing around about that — no way to misinterpret that. It's the very basis of our work. Our books provide this wonderful healing light through their inspired statements of spiritual truth.

For instance, isn't this a practical way of dealing with mortal error? Now, think of this carefully. It's in *Science and Health*: "The counter fact relative to any disease is required to cure it." Look at "required" there. It can mean the counter fact must cure the disease, or it can mean it is necessary for the cure — the counter fact. How often I've turned to this and begun the dissolution of the mortal claim by making a list of the "counter facts" of the specific lie, then going to the Concordance to learn more about each counter fact or truth. The wealth of specific truths just pours out and brings "the light of divine metaphysics" directly to bear. This is particularly effective when we feel overwhelmed or when mortal mind's opiate of apathy or discouragement suggests itself. This process may be almost mechanical at first, but soon the inspiration begins to flow. Sometime, when you feel overwhelmed about something, go to this method.

I'll give you an example. One weekend I had six heart attack cases. Three of them passed out on the phone. There was a lot of commotion going on. If you have a belief of a stomach ache or a headache, you think, well in a little while, it's going to be all right. But a heart attack? No! What's the fear? Death. What's the counter fact of death? Life! It's the only thing that is.

From my law days I always keep a pad by my desk, so I grabbed my pen. I'd never done this before. I began to write down the things that came to me as I thought about Life. That it was the counter fact of death. Energy. Vitality. Movement. Freedom. Strength. And so forth. These ideas came to me and pretty soon I exhausted every word I could think of. So I went and got my thesaurus. I took those words and I added to them. I got a couple of dictionaries. I used everything I could find to add to it. In the meanwhile, mortal mind was giving me a hard time. It said, "You'd better get busy, or you're going to have some dead patients."

By this time, I realized the power within this activity. You see, the search is sweet. What is your state of mind while you are looking for these counter facts of that lie? Spirituality — it's uplifting, buoying as you think of these things. I remember I had sixty-five words before I quit. I remember that one of them was "evergreen." Now maybe that didn't mean anything to anyone else, but to me it had a sort of freshness and vitality and renewing.

Anyway, I went to the Concordance and I looked up every word. Now, not everything fit, but the ideas that came flowing out of that book as I read about Life! I must have been four or five hours at that. By the time I finished, I had a clearer sense of Life than I had ever had before. The counter facts became reality. There could not be anything but Life when I finished. I felt that. By Monday morning, all six of them were back at work. Now, if I had been trying to fix cholesterol, or arteries, or valves, or something else, I could have been working still.

You see, it's this counter fact. And it's so simple to do. No matter how disturbed you are, you can get a pad, and you can begin to write these counter facts. Pretty soon, you see the fear quiet down, and pretty soon it's making sense to you. You read these tremendous statements pouring out from the books — beautiful thoughts! You never saw them like that before. The loveliness of them just comes out. We are blessed to have these books.

You know, Mrs. Eddy told us to look for her in her books. And sometimes, I say, when I'm by myself, "I'm coming for a visit with my dearest friend." I feel that way. That state of mind opens it up. It's exactly the state of mind you need in order to realize these spiritual facts. And as we do, the ideas just pour out. Or we work with Biblical truths such as, "Cease ye from man, whose breath is in his nostrils: for wherein is he to be accounted of." What does this say to mortal mind's demand to heal matter? "Cease ye."

We all know of these and hundreds of other familiar spiritual tools, and have used them often in our healing work. But it behooves us to be alert at the outset — at the first onslaught of mortal mind's picture. So we begin rightly from the spiritual premise, and we do not think we are using these spiritual truths to try to heal matter.

This is the constant challenge, isn't it? I've known people who have just spent years and years in the most earnest study. In fact every delayed healing I've ever seen has been principally because they went down the wrong path. Somehow or other they are trying to fix matter. Yet we know that the power we are dealing with is omnipotent. We have a right to expect this healing to come, because the power behind us is so much greater than anything before us. We have a right to feel this way.

Before we close, let me tell you the outcome of the real-life example we mentioned earlier. When the patient reported that every vestige of the cancer had vanished, for a moment I tried to think back a week to when I first saw her. I then realized that the important thing about this healing was that for the life of me, I could not remember seeing a single physical symptom or appearance of the problem, so completely free from matter had become my view of her. Not for one moment had there been an effort to heal or repair a material body. Every denial and affirmation was single-mindedly devoted to dissolving a lie and seeing in its place a perfect idea of God. I wish I could do this more consistently. It's a wonderful experience when you see this.

Her son was a close friend of the governor of California, and he had made personal arrangements for her to be examined by

16

the finest clinics in the state. Their diagnosis was unanimous — there was no way she could live. But that belief had no source, it had no substance in its lying claim — and there was no law to support it, known or unknown, medically or otherwise. With that you wipe the blackboard clean. Then you affirm what is true, and do that consistently.

Our Leader sets this forth in a statement you know so well, "Jesus beheld in Science the perfect man, who appeared to him where sinning mortal man appears to mortals. In this perfect man, the Saviour saw God's own likeness, and this correct view of man healed the sick." (*Science and Health*)

Healing is simply the practical application of the rules of this Science of the Christ, and beginning rightly is one of the rules. It is pretty well summed up in this statement: We're not trying to see mortal man as the image and likeness of God; we're trying to see the image and likeness of God instead of mortal man. Doesn't that make our goal in healing clear? And that's beginning rightly.

CHALLENGING HEREDITY

For untold centuries man has, in unthinking ignorance, accepted the package of "heredity" and lived with its contents unwittingly, and often unwillingly, but with a sense of resignation to the inevitable, good or bad.

We need to take a look at this "prize package," and take off its fancy wrappings, and see if it really is something that we want to accept and live with.

We are probably more aware than most of the tremendous concentration of world thought today on the mortal laws of heredity and genetics. But let me read you a few excerpts from some of the recent articles on this subject. In a science magazine directed largely to a medical group was this excerpt from an article dealing with genetics: "No one knows how many genetic diseases afflict man. As methods of studying human biochemistry take on new sophistication, scientists find themselves reluctantly adding names to the already long list of inherited disorders. Indeed, it has been estimated that as many as a quarter of all illnesses have a genetic component although they are by no means all directly heritable." (Leon E. Rosenberg of Yale University, "Finding and Treating Genetic Diseases." *Science News,* August 29, 1970)

An article in the *Wall Street Journal* entitled "The Chances Are . . ." says: "Two decades ago, several hundred disorders were known to stem from hereditary defects. Now medicine recognizes nearly fifteen hundred such ailments. And it is learning with increasing precision how they are passed from generation to generation." Hereditary disorders are becoming relatively more important to those concerned with the health of infants. It quotes Margaret W. Thompson, Genetic Counselor, as saying that "Fifty years ago about fifty percent of childhood deaths were caused by infectious diseases, and about two percent to three percent by diseases of known genetic origin. Now only one percent to two percent come from infectious diseases, while twelve percent result from ailments of known genetic origin."

In trying to do something about this, the medical profession is recommending that counselors obtain detailed family histories of both parents, extending if possible back to their grandparents. If the counselor finds a heredity defect in the history of the chromosomes of the parents, he calculates the odds that this defect might occur in the child, harking back to the laws of genetics first formulated by the Austrian Monk, Gregor Johan Mendel. Mr. Schacht of Minnesota believes the importance of genetic counseling is bound to increase because, he says, "As medical science salvages more and more people who otherwise would die of genetic disorders, they in turn will produce children with defective genes and our genetic problems are going to multiply." What a prophecy!

Some health specialists believe that it may become routine to examine a couple's genetic makeup before marriage, just as blood tests are administered now. There are stories similar to this almost daily in the newspapers and magazines. I cite these, not to rehearse or to stand aghast at error, but simply to expose it. Mrs. Eddy says in *Miscellaneous Writings*, "To know the what, when, and how of error, destroys error."

So now, in looking at this fallacious claim of heredity, let us look first to man's origin — the true and the false:

1. The only account of man's true origin is, of course, Genesis 1:26: " . . . created in the image and likeness of God." This absolute fact is the foundation of all our work in countering the false law of heredity.

2. The Adam and Eve story of the second chapter of Genesis, like so many tribal and religious fantasies offered over the centuries, was an attempt to answer the primitive tribesman's ques-

tions as to his origin. This account is, of course, not taken seriously today in any advanced scientific society.

3. But what of the Bible's third account of the creation in Genesis 4:1 — "And Adam knew Eve, and she conceived and bare Cain, and said, 'I have gotten a man from the Lord'"? Isn't this biological story of man's origin the very foundation of the world's belief in ancestry?

Enormous efforts have been made to confirm and support this biological base.

It was Darwin who offered an elaborate explanation of the first creation of the amino-acids — the single cell and its subsequent development into the present two-legged, two-armed, upright mortal, the Cro-Magnon man — what they say we are today. He said it occurred through "environment and conditioning"; or, as he termed it, "selective survival." Under this doctrine, of course, the claim is that these forces of "environment and conditioning" are constantly having their effect upon us today. When we look at or rehearse past experiences (our "conditioning") and accept their effect or impact upon ourselves or others, it is simply our acceptance of or submission to this baseless law of mortal mind, known as Darwin's Theory, isn't it?

Gregory Johan Mendel, the Austrian Monk, experimenting with garden peas, came up with the doctrine of inherited characteristics that he called "Mendel's Law of Heredity." It has, over the years, been expanded enormously from his simple claims of "dominant and recessive" genes, to include almost every aspect of man.

As you can see from the steady barrage of articles from medical science, almost at the moment of conception there is a combining of the genes of two parents that determine, they claim, almost everything about us: our body structure; our height; our coloring; our muscular development; our facial structure and appearance; our intelligence; our temperament; our criminal or peaceful tendencies; our athletic abilities; our artistic abilities; our very life span; and more recently, our susceptibility to an almost endless number of diseases.

In a recent criminal case, a man charged with a serious violent crime advanced as his defense, supported by considerable scientific testimony, that he was not responsible for his actions because of a certain deficiency in his genes — that because of this, he simply could not help it. The attempted defense was not successful, but it indicates the extent to which this doctrine is accepted.

Now, it is one thing to recognize, intellectually or theoretically, that these are the claims of "conditioning" and heredity, but to effectively stand guard at the portals of consciousness to keep them out appears to be quite difficult for most of us. Why? Well, just take a look at the "wrappings" of the packages they come in — so time-honored, pleasant, harmless, attractive — that few want to really look closely at them, but prefer to blink their mental eyes, and nicely rationalize or justify them as a kind of harmless little frailty or concession, and continue to accept the packages.

One of the most appealing packages is the birthday, isn't it? That special day when we are the star, the center of attention, when we are remembered so nicely! But what's in it? The reminding, the re-establishing that we are a biological creature, and thereby subject to the so-called laws of creation, environment, conditioning, heredity, known or unknown. Birthdays claim to be the starting point of a finite measurement called a life span, don't they? Whether one is conscious of it or not, all the limitations of the various stages of life are thereby actively declared against his well-being by the ignorant mass of universal thought. It has been said that the belief of death is the continuation of the belief of birth.

I know of an instance where a man had been suffering from what was termed an incurable fatal blood disease. He had turned from medicine to Christian Science when the doctors had given up and pronounced the death sentence. In discussing this with a practitioner one day, he mentioned with inordinate pride his ancestry traced from nobility in Europe, and as he spoke about it, it unfolded to the practitioner almost at once that it was this false belief of ancestry or heredity, that had to be handled. Immediate, specific work was done in this area, with the result that there was an immediate and total healing, and the man returned to robust health. Months later this man, in reading some old history books which had an account of his family, found that for generations the male members of his family had been dying from this same blood disease. You see, he didn't even know of it at the time, but he had accepted the "package" and all that it contained. Now, if he were an unknown orphan, and he and those around him were unaware of his parentage and race would this still affect him? There is no privilege of selection or discrimination allowed. We can't just accept the good — the others come with it. Whenever we accept this belief as a law, it appears to act as such. It often jumps several generations (if it is one of its so-called recessive characteristics) — something we could never have known of.

Isn't the same process concerned in the anniversaries of Mother's Day, Father's Day, and our other anniversaries which bring about a re-establishment of the passing of years? Looking back brings the various stages of the aging process and human birth into thought. We as Christian Scientists must be awake to the fact that material personality is not the real man, and ponder what the Master meant when he said, "Call no man your father upon earth. For one is your Father, which is in Heaven." Heredity is not a law of God, and belief in any phase of it indicates man's ignorance of his eternal, divine sonship. The man of God's creating, the only real man, is a living, loving, intelligent, wholly spiritual reflection of God. This man is without beginning or end, for the man God knows co-exists with Him *now*. And the awareness of this universal belief of ancestry puts us on our guard about even accepting the little harmless or pleasant-appearing effects of this so-called law. When people look at a new baby, they say that he has his father's nose, or his mother's disposition, or his grandmother's chin or dimple, on down to the last toenail. And we take pride at seeing the little partial replica of ourselves! And too, we've seen people exchange knowing looks when a child appears to express temper or some other family "curse." Did you ever notice it is always the other side of the family it comes from? Like the lady who said, "I didn't know how many faults my husband had until they began to come out in the children."

We cannot accept these effects without, at the same instant, accepting the cause, for the cause and the effect cannot be separated. If we accept a physical effect or condition as reality, as substance, we have accepted a material, mortal mind cause and its fallacious, devastating law.

Another one of the hydra-heads of this mortal mind serpent of birth is that of astrology. And it comes into effect when we declare a birthday. There are hundreds of millions of deluded believers of astrology today who are claiming a multitude of laws relative to each birthday. It is on almost every store counter, in every newspaper and magazine, asserting its baseless claims. It is even on computers now. This problem, too, rises from the belief in a material beginning, and is in the package, and therefore requires specific corrective work.

Mortal mind points with pride to a greater life expectancy, and how much this has come about through modern techniques. These life-expectancies are part of the law of probabilities which are so intimately associated with this law of inherited characteristics, where men take statistics, as do the insurance actuaries, and actually wager upon them, as in insurance policies. It is the law of probabilities that is a part of the whole false concept of ancestry which, if it is accepted, spells out the limits of our periods of activity. Isn't it ridiculous to time a man's capacity, his activities, his health, his appearance, all on how many trips the world has made around the sun, called years? Yet if, and I say if, these laws are accepted as facts, *we are as much under their domination as if they were facts.*

23

There's a story of a political prisoner in medieval times being placed in a dungeon and for twenty years was fed through a slot in an iron door. He never left his prison cell. And one day he tried the door, and to his amazement it swung open. It had never been locked. He walked by the guards and out into the sunlight unopposed. He had never been truly imprisoned during the entire time, except by his own acceptance of an illusion as a fact. And so it is with us, if we accept illusions as facts.

This is illustrated by a story: A hypochondriac told his doctor in great alarm that he had a fatal liver disease. "Nonsense," said the doctor. "You wouldn't know if you had it or not — there is no discomfort with that disease." "I know," gasped the patient, "that's my symptoms exactly."

If we enter into the great conspiracy of heredity and the hypnotic beliefs connected with it, they have the effect of fact, even though they are illusion. How can a knowledge of this assist us right now, right where we are, in a better expression of harmony and activity and joy and strength and agility? Well, the answer lies within our own consciousness, doesn't it? How willing are we to part with this concept of body and its origin, and to replace it with the spiritual concept?

I am reminded of a little girl in Sunday School. When she was told what she could expect when she went to heaven, she cried and said, "But I don't want to go. I like hamburgers and movies." So often, consciously or unconsciously, we cling to what we consider the pleasurable aspect of the laws of heredity and the fond maternalism and paternalism, unwilling to seek genuinely a greater spiritualization of our thought. Often we simply want to be more comfortable in matter. As one French philosopher put it, "Everyone wants to live longer, but no one wants to grow old."

The limitations on our spiritual development, on our turning loose of this false law and any of its claims, good or bad, are dependent on our willingness to release them and let them go. One doesn't have to pick up that package, but there must be a willingness not to, and an alertness to its description and its deceptions. How does the temporary pleasure of a birthday party, Mother's Day, Father's Day, anniversaries, all the gifts and attention, really compare with the freedom from the process of aging, from the fastening of false laws of immaturity, lack of judgment, carelessness, on the young, and the limitations of decrepitude on the mature? Too young or too old? What fallacies! Since when did an idea of God, an eternal idea, become old or young? "The measurement of time by solar years robs youth and gives ugliness to age," Mrs. Eddy says in *Science and Health.* "Robs youth," she says, and truly it does. So it is important to our children and our grandchildren, as it is to us, that this birthday ritual be properly handled, and its claims reversed so that they shall not be robbed of their true productivity, harmony, opportunities of expression. For the claim of aging starts, of course, at the earliest of ages. "Oh well, a little birthday party and some nice gifts won't hurt them, and they enjoy it so, and all the other kids are having them." It's not hard to rationalize about it, but is it really the highest sense of love of which we are capable?

How about the common practice of guessing or surmising the age of the people we meet, sometimes audibly, but more often to oneself? This is the kind of reciprocal malpractice which is harmful to all concerned. Yet, if we are not aware of it, it slips in on us as one of these innocuous habits which keeps one enslaved — a recurring type of hypnotic suggestion. Mrs. Eddy was very definite about this. "Never record ages," she says. "Time tables of birth and death are so many conspiracies against manhood and womanhood." (*Science and Health*)

In *Miscellany* Mrs. Eddy says: "Is God infinite? Yes. Did God make man? Yes. Did God make all that was made? He did. Is God Spirit? He is. Did infinite Spirit make that which is not spiritual? No. Who or what made matter? Matter as substance or intelligence was never made. Is mortal man a creator, is he matter or spirit? Neither one. Why? Because Spirit is God and infinite; hence there can be no other creator and no other creation. Man is but His image and likeness. Are you a Christian Scientist? I am. Do you adopt as truth the above statements? I do. Then why this meaningless commemoration of birthdays, since there are none?"

She continues: "Had I known what was being done in time to have prevented it, that which commemorated in deed or word what is not true, would never have entered into the history of our church buildings. Let us have no more of echoing dreams."

Age is one of the most persistent diseases in human belief. People believe they get over other diseases, but do they really believe they get over the belief of age? Or the concept that they must die from it? *We should start now in handling the belief of age* — totally, without the thought that it is beyond us, that death is unavoidable, like taxes, or that there are many things we should handle before this! We should recognize now that life is inevitable. You *cannot* escape it — no matter what you do. Declare the counter fact that "*life is inevitable*," rather than "death is inevitable." Do this regularly. *Life is unavoidable!* This is the declaration of the counter fact. This understanding, which is itself so alive that it could not possibly believe in anything contrary to its aliveness, will help to handle the belief of death. So our work is to declare daily the inevitability, the unavoidability, the eternality of the life that is you – God's life. Every time a suggestion of aging or inactivity is presented to us or to anyone else, review the qualities of life — one at a time, if necessary. This is immediately effective.

Perhaps our denial of heredity may include some of these thoughts:

1. I was never born, therefore I can never die.
2. I am not Spirit encapsuled in flesh or a sack of skin. I am all Spirit.
3. I am not a "biological" accident, but a purposeful, intelligent, harmonious idea of God.
4. I am not predestined except to express Mind which created me.

5. I am not subject to any so-called laws of ancestry or heredity, known or unknown, individual or universal. I am guided, controlled, directed, sustained by the law of Mind which created me — the only law.
6. I am under no family "curse" — no line of development nor ancestry. As God's child, I am His heir — heir to every quality and function of God.
7. I am not a mortal child or parent. I am a divine idea from a perfect Father-Mother God, as are all of His children.
8. There is no law of astrology or the zodiac, and I am not subject to its false signs or superstitions. There is no law but God's law.
9. There is no occultism, witchcraft, nor orientalism — it cannot come nigh my dwelling. I dwell in the "secret place of the most high" at peace in the kingdom of heaven.
10. I am not subject to the aggressive mental suggestion of others known or unknown, individual or collective. I cannot be influenced or subject to the thinking of others, nor will I accept into consciousness what I think others are thinking — or fear it. I can be influenced by nothing but God, good, and I know it. And I know I know it.

Now, let's sum up this false dream of ancestry: Man is not born from the dust of the ground, nor is he a biological descendent of protoplasm. He is not bound about with fetters of hereditary laws and genetic rules, not at the mercy of genes and chromosomes. No superstitions of astrology or preordination can by ignorant, popular acceptance become a law unto him. In short, man simply is not in nor of a body of matter, regardless of all the sense testimony, history, or human statistics. Man made in the image and likeness of God is spiritual.

Spiritual consciousness precedes birth. Life has no beginning, no interruptions, no ending. Life is not the result of something. It is the cause of all things!

The whole issue of ancestry and heredity really brings to light a most important aspect of healing — that of being willing to turn loose of a cherished human belief. The mental limitations held secretly will, of course, limit our present demonstrations proportionately. But isn't it wonderful to know that regardless of what we think of man (ourselves), no matter how limited or distorted our views are, it isn't going to change or even slightly affect what God created: our perfection, our eternality! All, absolutely all, that our thoughts can change or affect is simply our view of man. Now let's go forward and rise to a better view!

PRACTICAL WISDOM

When I was asked to discuss practical wisdom, it seemed to me a very appropriate thing. So, I began to consider these two words. I looked in the dictionary for the definition of the word *practical* and it says, "that which is useful and makes good sense"— and *wisdom* is defined as "knowledge and good judgments based on experience; wise conduct." Now, these definitions would seem to have a very special application to Christian Science practice. We are going to discuss a very special application of practicality — "There is no matter." This probably is the most radical statement the world has ever known in a material sense. Let's stop and think what Mrs. Eddy said about this in *Miscellany*, in the last paragraph of her letter to the churches in New York, "There is no matter is not only the axiom of true Christian Science, it is the only basis upon which this Science may be demonstrated."

If there ever was a strong, clear-cut statement, that's it! There is no equivocation. There is no room for any compromise in regard to that. It must be the basic frame of reference. It must be the basic attitude — the feeling that a Christian Scientist must have in order to do the most effective healing work. There is no sick matter; there is no well matter; there is no old matter; there is no young matter; there is no pink matter; there is no white matter; there is no diseased matter; there is no healthy matter; there is no bad matter; there is no good matter. And we have to see that matter doesn't matter — and to do it consistently.

Most of you have gone onto roadways and airways, and you have traveled many thousands of miles. Yet I submit — you never went anywhere! You see, when we know there is no matter, we know there is no space, because space is only the distance between material objects, and if there are no material objects, there

29

is no space. There is no separation. There is unity of thought, which, when we get some concept of this, we can understand how Jesus could move the whole boatload of men three and one-half miles across the water instantly, how he could walk through walls, how there was no material impediment to his movements, because he recognized that there was no matter.

This is a very radical stand because the whole world is saying that we live in matter, that we are dependent upon it. It says that Spirit entered into a capsule of flesh and has stayed there for so many trips around the sun — we call them years — and then it leaves to go to someplace — heaven, hell, some place. All are theories. But it says that body is a temporary dwelling place of Spirit! In reducing this to the ultimate, you can see how ridiculous it is. It would place God in a position of dependency. Omnipotent God, omnipresent God, in a position of dependency upon the whim and fancy of two mortals getting together, having sexual relations, having a baby born in order that there would be a house that Spirit could dwell in. Isn't that the most ridiculous concept you could possibly imagine? *Man is spiritual.* The first story of creation is the *only* story of creation. The second story, Adam and Eve, the allegory for the tribesmen, nobody really takes too seriously. But, that third story of creation: " . . . and Adam knew Eve and she conceived and bare Cain and said, I have gotten a man from the Lord," this biological story of creation, has placed us in this false concept about birth which has continued and has kept us chained to a matter-body as something. The only possible way we will ever be free of death is to understand there was no birth, that there is no matter.

In regard to being practical. It is going to come to you sometime in facing severe challenges that you have to use wisdom. How many times do you hear that from Christian Scientists? Of course you do; there is no question about it. But wisdom cannot be exercised at the expense of radical Christian Science. Our mission is to heal, and there is no healing unless we are radical Christian

Scientists! No way! When these suggestions come to us, realize what Mrs. Eddy said — that this is the only basis upon which Christian Science may be demonstrated. There is no room for quibbling about it. And of course, the reason we have to be practical, radical Christian Scientists, and why radicalism is the most practical thing, is because *it heals*.

Now mind you, it's your state of mind we are talking about. I'm not saying that you are not going to take good physical care of yourself; but what is the state of mind? You don't have to worry about whether the practitioners are going to do the kind, loving, practical, wise thing if their state of mind is right. That will follow automatically. You don't have to give them specific instructions about being loving and understanding and caring, about quieting fears, when they understand the mythical nature of the whole sense testimony. When that is in their hearts, there will be no problem about their practical demonstration of it. And speaking about being practical — was it practical to go fishing when Caesar's tax had to be paid? Was it practical to invite thousands of people to a picnic when you have two fishes and five loaves? Was it practical to let someone lie dead for four days in the desert heat before you even tried to heal them? Was it practical to personal sense to turn down a kingdom to be crucified on the cross? But with such acts of radical practicality, Jesus changed the lives of more people than anybody who has ever lived, and will do so in the future. It is that kind of radical practicality which will enable you to change the lives of more people. It means that you can bring your healing mission to untold thousands of people in the most practical way possible.

We speak in the relative to be understood of men, but we think in the absolute to understand God, and our thinking is what we are talking about here. We must think in the absolute. I'll never forget the comments of a little practitioner I knew, who in her late 90's was still making housecalls. She didn't have any concept about age being a limitation at all. I remember when she used to get ready to go to bed, she would say, "Well, I have to bathe my doll now and

31

put it to bed." That is the way she regarded this whole thing about body. Earlier in her life, she had been condemned by the medical people to be a helpless cripple the rest of her life and would never leave a wheelchair. She had been told that she would never be able to read because of eye problems — but she didn't believe them! She demonstrated an activity which was just beautiful, because she looked past matter, and that is the crux of the whole thing.

Mrs. Eddy says that in metaphysics we "resolve things into thoughts and exchange the objects of sense for the ideas of Soul." You don't see a table — you are aware of a thought of a table. It has no reality. It does not exist, except as a mental image — absolutely nothing else! This reinforced concrete building that we think we are sitting in is entirely composed of thought — that's all! If we start to think this way, it isn't such a big task to take the next step and realize that this $3.65 worth of chemicals that we call body is 86% water, and 3 1/4 pounds of gray matter in a cranial cavity is supposed to be the origin of thought. It becomes somewhat ridiculous. I remember Paul Stark Seeley saying that if you could squeeze all the space out between the electrons and protons in the atomic structure of the body, you would have a speck so tiny that you could not see it on the point of a pin. And that's the solid stuff we talk about? Recently in the *Examiner* there was an article by atomic physicists in which they were openly stating that matter resolves itself to nothing but crystallized thought. There is no question about it — to the atomic physicists that is all it amounts to, and that's all we are seeing. We can't stand aghast at nothingness!

Now, how do we make this appearance of matter into a no-thing and keep it a no-thing. What is the process? What is the best way of doing this? Mrs. Eddy said in the thirty-second edition of *Science and Health*, "Sleep and mesmerism explain the mythical nature of material sense." So let's think about that for a moment. If we can once see the mythical nature of what appears to be matter, we are never going to stand so much aghast of it again.

It means that when you walk down the street, and you see a tree, or a bird, or an automobile, you can stop and think, "That's a thought of a tree; it's a thought of a bird. It all exists in thought." I find myself practicing this because, in that first step of what Mrs. Eddy says about resolving things into thought, there is the difficulty. The world is holding before us constantly the concept that this is reality, and Mrs. Eddy's way of using sleep and hypnotism as the illustrations of the nothingness of this is so wise.

Let's take a dream for instance. In a dream we see, we feel, we hear, we have all the physical sense reports — sometimes more vividly than we do in a waking experience. And yet we know that everything we beheld, everything we experienced, was entirely in thought. Not one single aspect of the dream was ever anything but thought, and we know that. But when we awake into what we call this waking experience, we say, "Oh, but this is real." But this is just as mythical, just as much a dream, as that sleeping experience. And when we realize that we are only dealing with thought in the waking experience, just as much as we are in the dream, we'll begin to deal with thought. As long as we are dealing with it as matter, we don't get into the ballgame. You've got to resolve things into thought before you can begin to make the exchange, and the exchange only takes place after you have it in the area of thought. That is why the practice of seeing things as thought puts it in the area where you can say, "Well, big deal!" But if you see it as something where cell structure has to be changed, an organ has to be restored, all of a sudden you are in a different ballgame. This is what the world is holding before your view constantly. An understanding of the mythical nature of matter enables you *not* to stand aghast.

Let's look at it through hypnotism, and you are going to see ultimately that hypnotism is all you are ever dealing with. It is no accident that Mrs. Eddy says that animal magnetism is hypnotism, because that really explains what it is — often *unconsciously* induced. Most of us believe that for anyone to become hypnotized there has to be somebody with black glassy eyes that fix upon you and hold your attention as you are watching the pendulum or bright light or swirling circle, thereby bringing you under his Svengali control. Believe me, this is not true. This thing of voluntary hypnotism does not require even a spoken word. It has been proven that hypnotists can influence the thoughts of people thousands of miles away. There is not a single group of people in the world trained to handle this except Christian Scientists. We have to realize the mental nature of things and the power of hypnotic control.

I would like to tell you how to deal with this, which I think you will find helpful. A man whom I know had a very good friend who was an expert hypnotist; they used to talk metaphysics from time to time. He used to say to the Scientist: "One of these days I'm going to hypnotize you, then you will understand what we are talking about — the power this has." The Scientist used to rather good naturedly scoff at this.

Time went on, and one night they went to dinner in the Persian Room of St. Francis Hotel in San Francisco. The Scientist ordered lamb chops. Presently the waitress served him. He looked down at his plate and said, "Just a minute, Miss. You've made a mistake in my order. I ordered lamb chops, not watermelon." She said, "What watermelon?" "Well," he said, "this watermelon." He held up the big slab of red watermelon right there in front of him. She said, "Are you trying to put me on?" "Well, no — I'm talking about this. I know that I ordered lamb chops!" She said, "Well, I served you lamb chops. That's what you've got!" They got into quite an argument and finally he caught a glimpse of his friend sitting across from him with a little smirk on his face. He stopped and looked right at him, and he said, "You finally did it, didn't you?" And that broke the spell! He looked back at his plate and there, where an instant before there had been a big slab of watermelon, there were the lamb chops. So he rather shamefacedly excused himself with the waitress, and they went on with their meal.

The next day he and his mother went to visit an invalid aunt

34

who was suffering from a belief of cancer of the face. She had reached the stage where she could no longer go out in public, so the family took turns visiting; this day was their turn. He had shared the experience about the watermelon with his mother before they went. As they walked into the aunt's room, he caught a glimpse of her face all covered with this growth. He turned to his mother, almost with a chuckle, and said, "Why, Auntie has watermelon all over her face." He saw so clearly that it was absolutely hypnotic — it was not actual. There was no reality in it, and he saw it and his mother saw it. They then talked to the aunt about what body really is. The next morning the niece who was taking care of the aunt called — so excited she could scarcely speak. She said, "The most wonderful thing has just happened! That entire cancerous growth just fell off of auntie's face this morning and she is *well!*"

Let's look for a moment at what happened. In psychology they have come to recognize that the breaking of a hypnotic spell requires two steps. The first step is recognizing it to be an illusion. Now, isn't that exactly what happened when the man turned to his friend and said, "You finally did it"? You see, at that instant he had recognized that it was illusion. Now, you must recognize it to be an illusion, even when you are still standing knee-deep in it. Even though that watermelon was still there when he said it, he recognized it to be an illusion. That is what we must do. Even though it looked like that cancerous growth was all over her face, he recognized it to be an illusion, when he turned to his mother and said, "Why, Auntie's got watermelon all over her face."

The second step which is required is to know what the fact is. That's what the waitress had provided in the first instance, hadn't she? She said, "Those are lamb chops." See, she had provided the fact right there. The combination of those two things had to break the spell. With the aunt, when she recognized what true body is, what the fact was — that she was spiritual, every whit spiritual, not one iota matter — it had to break the spell. There was no way it could be avoided. Absolutely no way! It is as unavoidable as darkness disappearing when light is placed in it's presence. The oldest, most enduring darkness you could possibly imagine in a cave that had been dark for ten million years, would give way instantly before the light of a tiny little flashlight.

A lie, in the presence of the truth, is absolutely lost! Our job is to stand in the midst of the illusion and declare it's illusory nature — claiming it to be a lie, a mental imagery and nothing more. We have to see things as thought, a hypnotic thought, in order to exchange the objects of sense for the ideas of Soul. When that happens, there is no avoidance of healing. You are really only revealing that which was there all the time. From the human picture, those lamp chops were there all the time.

> *When mortal mind is talking.*
> *And lifts its hydra head,*
> *I don't have to listen,*
> *'Cause nothing's being said.*

We never heal conditions; we just remove false beliefs from consciousness. Mrs. Eddy says in *Miscellaneous Writings*, "Every material belief hints at the existence of spiritual reality." Stop and realize that there has to be a spiritual idea, and that every material object is simply a misconception of it. Now, here is a fountain pen; it looks like a fountain pen; it feels like one. It seems useful, purposeful. But this is a thought of a pen. Now, that's my first step. I see it as a thought — a material thought. Where did that thought have its origin? We know there is only one Mind — that Mind is the source of all, totally all. There is no other Mind. Then, that means the thought had to have its origin in the Divine Mind. As a fountain pen? I don't know. It is visible only through the material senses, but it is a divine idea that has been distorted through the lens of personal sense (we call it the human mind), and it comes out looking like a fountain pen. Some of the qualities of that divine idea came through that distorting lens — strength, balance, symmetry, grace, utility — enough things so that it is a useful instrument. But imagine what the real is like! Isn't it an exciting thing to think that we'll come to see this as our thought is uplifted? We look at a sunset and we think, "Isn't it magnificent?" But imagine the beauty of the spiritual idea when we behold it in its reality, when we can see it in the spiritual sense completely. Mrs. Eddy says that these ideas have form, color and outline. This gives us some idea of what Mrs. Eddy means when she said, "I love your promise," and it does hold such a beautiful promise of what's real.

Now I would like to share with you another thing about hypnotism. I think it is the most excellent example on the necessity for continuity that I know of. This came from Laura Sargent, and I think it explains something of what is demanded of us in our work. During Mrs. Eddy's time, one of her students anxious to know more about the handling of animal magnetism, took passage for India. He wanted to learn more about the defenses to mesmerism. He took his things aboard the ship and put them away in his room, and then he went upon the deck to watch the stevedores load the boat. There were great stacks of boxes sitting all over the docks in big orderly piles, and everyone was happily going about their business.

Among the passengers he met a Hindu, and they started talking. Pretty soon he spoke to the Hindu and said, "Do you believe in mesmerism?" Well, it was a beautiful sunny day, but all of a sudden the most terrible storm came in from the Atlantic. Great waves smashed into that boat and threw it like a toy against the docks. The wind knocked those big piles of crates around, knocked some of the stevedores off into the water. Great waves piled up under the piers and tore the roof off of some of the buildings. The men had to hold on for dear life to the railing of the boat to keep from being thrown overboard. It was a frightening experience! Just the most terrible forces!

This went on for some time. Then, just as quickly it stopped. It absolutely stopped! The fellow looked down at the dock, and there were the stevedores going on about their business just as quietly as before. All the crates were standing there in perfect order. No roofs were torn off; the water as calm as a lake, and the Hindu turned to him and said, "I've just answered your question." Well, he went on with his trip. He arrived in India and he kept his appointment with the adept who was to teach him about mesmerism. He was shown into his quarters. They were very sparsely furnished — just a table and chair. He was left alone. Presently, the door opened and a man came in carrying a magnificent big Indian vase. He had never seen anything so beautiful! He walked around in front of him and suddenly lifted the vase over his head and slammed it on the floor with all of his force. It broke into a thousand pieces — that beautiful vase! It was a startling experience, but the Scientist was a bit prepared for this because of his experience in the boat. He remembered what the Hindu had told him, "The only defense against mesmerism is to hold to a fact; no matter how simple it is, hold to a fact." The only fact that came to him right at the moment was 2 x 2 = 4; and he held to it. To his amazement, the vase and all of its pieces disappeared from view. Absolutely disappeared! He was alone in the room. Well, he sat back, kind of proud of himself for what he had been able to accomplish. He allowed his thought to kind of drift away and when he did, instantly it was back — the whole mess all over the floor. He stopped and went back to that fact again. It disappeared again. He sat there a little bit and pretty soon let his thought wander and back it came again. In and out — in and out. Finally, he saw he had to maintain that fact. And he did. And with that, the vase disappeared permanently. The door opened, and the mesmerist came in and said, "You never need fear mesmerism again. You now know the secret of dealing with it."

Mrs. Sargent told her students this in order to illustrate the point of the necessity of continuity in our work. You can't just know the nothingness of a lie and then let yourself drift back into it again. In our Sunday Schools we teach the basic treatment of denial and affirmation. That is what we're doing. We are breaking the mental state. I very seldom use the word "healing" in my own thinking because it is hard for me to keep the thought of healing separate from a gradual process of a deep wound closing and something happening. But if I think of "revealing" — no problem. I am only seeing what is there already. I am not having to change anything. It is already there as fact.

The ten lepers were healed, not when they stood in the presence of Jesus, but when they stood in the presence of what he knew. Let your patients stand in the presence of what you know. When you are tempted to believe what you see, remember the experience of the practitioner when faced with the dreadfulness of a disease, who said, "Father, you were there — what did you see?" Stop and think about that. It is helpful because when we see it through those eyes, the dreadfulness of the appearance, the helplessness, the hopelessness, the world belief of incurability is utterly washed away. Have confidence. Some Christian Scientists I've known are a lot like tea bags. Their real strength does not come out until they get into hot water!

Now, to sum it up: Be radical Christian Scientists! It's only radical as far as the world standards are concerned. It is the most practical wisdom on earth. Know that there is no matter. *Really know it! Feel it! Think it!* Remember, it's the feel of it that counts. Work with great love toward Jesus and love toward Mrs. Eddy. There has to be love — love of Mrs. Eddy, love of Jesus. Read some of the biographies so that you come to have this feeling about her. It is so important. Because when we love her, all the rest of it opens up. If you come to feel this, it makes all the difference in the world.

OUR ORIGINAL IDENTITY

"How old would you be if you didn't know how old you are?" A friend of mine had this thought-provoking question put to her by her son. If you were asked this question, how would you answer? Think about it for a moment.

Down through the ages, with all too few exceptions, mankind has bowed its head in blind submission to the false laws of time and aging. Time has been accepted as inevitable, irresistible. Material sense, based on this claimed force, outpictures human life as having a beginning, as briefly flourishing, then disintegrating. This is life as mortal mind conceives of it — finite, measurable, going through stages and inevitably ending.

This sense of life is based on the so-called laws of mortal mind, often referred to as laws of nature or natural laws. Considered as laws of nature, they appear to have the power, authority, absoluteness, and finality of rules established and enforced by God, for almost everyone accepts that God made every so-called natural thing. But such a blind acceptance of the concept that anything bearing the description natural must be God-originated, tends to have us accept it as unavoidable, as so-called law. Stop and think — aren't we inclined to do this? Isn't that the bland answer given so often to even some mortal mind activity of gross sensuality and materiality, no matter how savage or brutal it may be, as in the law of the jungle? "Oh, that's the law of nature," we say.

Based on this preliminary misconception of a divine origin, mankind is often inclined to accept as unavoidable the so-called natural laws of biological life: birth, maturing, aging, disease, disintegration, and death, because an error in the premise always leads to an error in the conclusion.

These so-called natural laws are all based on the founda-

40

tion of biological birth, for it all starts here. As an ancient Latin proverb states: "We start to die when we are born, and the end depends on the beginning."

So let's look at birth. And what better place to start than with the Bible's three accounts of creation.

The first chapter of Genesis states that man is made in the image and likeness of God — totally spiritual. This is, of course, the only true story of creation.

The second account of creation is written simply as an allegory for the spiritually ignorant tribesman. It is in the second chapter of Genesis. Scarcely anyone accepts this account as factual. I doubt that anyone here really believes that they came from a rib or a pinch of dust.

But what of that third account, the biological, so-called natural story of creation: " . . . and Adam knew Eve his wife; and she conceived, and bare Cain, and said, I have gotten a man from the Lord." This attributes material creation to God, and the world, almost everyone in it, learns and accepts this as the true story of man's creation. Why, of course, it's natural, isn't it?

Based on this false law, other so-called laws dealing with nature are pronounced and accepted — such as laws of inheritance, and Mendel's laws of material genetics, which were, interestingly enough, propounded by an Austrian monk in 1866, the very year of Mrs. Eddy's discovery of the divine laws of Christian Science. Isn't that significant — the genuine and the counterfeit? Though greatly enlarged, Mendel's laws are today taught the world over as being the genetically controlling laws in all living things. We know them as laws of ancestry or inheritance, and for the most part, accept them without much question — as being natural.

For example, if a mother-to-be has red hair, and her husband has red hair, what color do you confidently expect the baby's hair to be? Or if they both are tall, don't we expect their children to be tall? And so on, with dozens of bodily characteristics, including their life-span. Why do you think life insurance companies ask you

41

all those questions about your family and how long they lived? Because they believe that it has something to do with your life span. They may not call it Mendel's law in operation, but that's what it is technically known as.

Also we speak of the inexorable effect of environment and conditioning on all living things — Darwin's law, another so-called material law of nature. And you submit yourself to this false law, whether you want to or not, when you pick up the package of material birth.

If we were to ask which story of creation is true — the first, man as spiritual, or the third, the biologically based material account, most Christian Scientists would answer, "Well, of course, the first, for man is spiritual." We say it all the time, don't we? But are we living it, and really identifying ourselves with it? Our textbook, *Science and Health*, makes so clear the importance of this concept: "The foundation of mortal discord is a false sense of man's origin."

Mrs. Eddy does not say that this "false sense of man's origin" is "a" foundation or "one" of the foundations, but "*the*" foundation of mortal discord." Think of this. She says that "mortal discord" is founded upon this false sense! Yet I would not want to ask how many are (for themselves or others) still celebrating — actually celebrating — a day honoring a material origin: something which our Leader referred to as "the foundation of mortal discord!" And she was certainly specific in her directions about this. Here is what she says in *Science and Health*: "Never record ages. Chronological data are no part of the vast forever. Time-tables of birth and death are so many conspiracies against manhood and womanhood."

Perhaps the most subtle activities of all (in denying God as the creator of man) are Mother's Day and Father's Day. Their beautiful verses, cards, sentiments, are delightful. I always loved to shop for them and later enjoyed receiving them. But we can see how they specifically establish the recognition and acceptance of our material origin, and with it all the dreaded false laws of aging, genetics, and conditioning for ourselves and our loved ones. For doesn't what looks like (and is certainly intended as) the sweetest act of kindness and appreciation serve to fasten on and subjugate our loved ones to these cruel, destructive laws of aging, weakness, deterioration, and death. It comes, of course, in the guise of love and gratitude in order to get past our guard.

These wonderful right motives can still be joyously exercised by having "special days," or, as some articles term them, "no days" — times of individual recognition, gratitude, and love. Such sweet surprises, held on another day, do not re-establish a false material basis for man. Isn't this an even higher sense of love?

Ask any experienced practitioner how often he has calls from patients closely following a birthday celebration, or Mother's Day, or Father's Day. Why? Because of an unintended reinforcing of the suggestion of aging, with all of its false natural laws of limitation and finiteness. For when the party is over and everyone has gone home, the honored guest is left alone to consider, "I am getting older." And all the dreaded contemplation of what that means begins to set in.

Even with youth, it re-establishes the imposed limitations of lack of judgment, experience, coordination, and reason. In fact, I would like to ask you a question. Under these material laws and their restrictions, what is the perfect age? You should have heard the opinions when I asked my Sunday School class of college students this question. But they finally agreed that we are always too young or too old. There simply is no "optimum age" from a material viewpoint.

We come to see that Mrs. Eddy's directions to us in the exercise and demonstration of this Science of the Christ all have purpose — a divine purpose — and so do her directives regarding birth. Consider the importance that Jesus attached to this. *The Christian Science Journal* of December 1946, cites a Biblical historian who reported the Master as saying: "I am come to destroy the works of birth." Jesus never was much of a compromiser with material birth. Should we be, when we see what we have to expect from it?

In sharp contrast to the world's accepted third story of material birth (and its inevitable laws of aging and decay), let's look at man's existence under the first chapter of Genesis — the first and true story of man's origin. Mrs. Eddy puts it so clearly in a statement you know well: "God expresses in man the infinite idea forever developing itself, broadening and rising higher and higher from a boundless basis." (Science *and Health*) What a different view of man, this spiritual one! Birthless, and therefore ageless!

But what is age? Where is age located? In body? Of course not. Even the doctors have come to see this in their study of anatomy. Age is only a collection of false, educated beliefs — simply images of mortal thought reflected on the retina of human consciousness. These false mental images are what the world interprets as age. Age is never a condition with which we have to deal. There is never a matter body which has to be reconstituted. I repeat: Age is not a physical condition; it is only a mental suggestion which has been accepted and thereby has become a belief — all in thought! Age has also been described as simply an accumulation of unhandled beliefs.

The false education of mortal mind's suggestions that we have carelessly accepted, has taught us wrongly; and so man has appeared to himself to age and die in obedience to his mental acceptance of these suggestions of age, but certainly not because of a physical condition. Seeing all of these material-appearing symptoms of aging as belief or suggestion, rather than as physical conditions, is imperative. May I illustrate?

When we begin by looking at man according to the first story of creation, as spiritual, then we can see clearly that neither the suggestion of heredity or disease of any kind could ever be true of a spiritual idea. It follows so surely when this is the basis of our identification of man.

We can gain a little insight into the continuous freedom afforded by simply beginning with the Genesis account of spiritual man, the image and likeness of God, in drawing our conclusions about ourselves. How enormously important this is to our well being and spiritual growth for, as Mrs. Eddy said, "To begin rightly is to end rightly." (*Science and Health*)

We come to see that identifying ourselves as the "image and likeness of God" establishes not only our perfection, harmony, joy, intelligence, divine purpose, strength and freedom, but it establishes our *immortality* and all that it includes. We see ourselves as birthless, and therefore ageless, deathless, diseaseless, and indestructible, as "never born and never dying." Our Leader tells us: "The human capacities are enlarged and perfected in proportion as humanity gains the true conception of man and God." (*Science and Health*)

Is there anyone who wouldn't want their "human capacities enlarged and perfected"? Isn't that what we are all seeking? This is, of course, exactly what this identification of ourselves as God's image and likeness does.

This identification requires consistency in looking to the spiritual model. If we don't, we are like a sculptor carving a statue of a kangaroo. Every other day a prankster who knows the sculptor to be a little forgetful, puts a picture of a wart hog on the easel where the picture of the kangaroo had been. The sculptor fails to notice, and goes busily on with his work. One day he looks at a kangaroo model — the next day at a wart hog model. You can well imagine the odd statue that evolves! Probably the highest jumping two-legged hog that you ever heard of!

How about the mental switching which goes on in the identification of ourselves — one hour as an idea of God, looking to and through the spiritual sense to the spiritual model, and the next hour slipping over and seeing ourselves as mortal, looking to and through physical sense at the matter model, having a material birth. Is it any wonder that we become discouraged, confused, and tired with the result? Isn't this all that goes on with dualism, trying to serve two masters — Spirit and matter? When we try to cling to both, we are like a man going down on a sinking ship and holding desperately to its main mast. Then when someone on a rescue ship throws him a rope, he tries to play it safe by holding onto it as well as to the mast — one with each hand — it almost tears him in two! Sooner or later we, too, have to make our choice — a matter model of man born unto woman or the spiritual model, God's man.

Annie M. Knott, one of Mrs. Eddy's early students, gives us an interesting concept of choosing the right model, (*Christian Science Sentinel,* January 10, 1914). Here is a section: "In one of Mrs. Eddy's classes, a student remarked that she always endeavored to have the perfect body in her thought when giving a treatment. Mrs. Eddy at once asked where she found her authority for such a method. The student hesitatingly responded that it was from *Science and Health*, and after a little search she triumphantly read the statement on page 407, 'Let the perfect model be present in your thoughts.' Smiling, as one would at the mistake of a child, Mrs. Eddy then asked if she regarded the body as the 'model' here referred to, and the student said she had so believed up to that moment. With the utmost patience Mrs. Eddy then explained to her students that we can only perceive the divine and perfect model as we are, to quote Paul, 'absent from the body' and 'present with the Lord.' Humanity has been slowly yielding up the belief in a corporeal God, but it still clings to the belief in a bodily model for man, while accepting the scriptural statement that he is God's likeness. Strictly speaking, we can have but one model, God's perfect idea, with countless reflections, all governed by the one divine Principle." So we see how important it is for us to have an ageless, spiritual model and to look at it continually, as Mrs. Eddy says.

In closing — what do we have a right to expect from holding to such a spiritual model? Someone well past middle-age might ask, "Is it too late for me?" Let Mrs. Eddy answer this in her response to a similar question published in *The Christian Science Journal* (vol.2, No. 9, page 3): "Is it possible to change the aged form to one of youth, beauty and immortality, without the change called death?" Mrs. Eddy replied, "In proportion as the law of Truth is understood and accepted, it obtains in person and character. The deformities and infirmities said to be the inevitable results of age, under the opposite mental impressions, disappear. You change the physical manifestation in proportion to your changed thoughts of the effect of accumulative years. Expecting an increase of usefulness and vigor from advanced years with as much faith as you look for decrepitude and ugliness, a favorable result would be sure to follow. The added wisdom of age and experience is strength, not weakness, and we should understand this, expect it, and know that it is so, then it would appear.'"

Think of it! We are birthless, ageless, deathless, and we live progressively ascending all the time!

Every day is your birthday dear,
Every day throughout the year
Your loving Father gives to you
A birthday gift, all fresh and new:
Joyous life that cannot cease,
Blessed Truth that giveth peace,
Love that doth all good increase.
Every day is your birthday dear,
Every day throughout the year.

SPIRITUAL RADICALISM

Some of us, particularly those of us who think of ourselves as quiet, non-violent, "honor thy father and thy mother," honest, law-abiding conservatives, would hardly think of ourselves as radicals. But our very presence here today gives us away as just that — radicals, in the truest sense of the word.

The origin of the word *radical* comes, as you might expect, from the Latin *radix* or *root*. When we embraced Christian Science, we subscribed to the very roots of the Science of Christianity, which Jesus stated clearly when he said, "God is a Spirit: and they that worship him must worship him in spirit and in truth."

Christian Science is essentially this same radicalism. In writing to the New York churches, Mrs. Eddy set forth the position of her church in the boldest language possible. She said, "Spirit is infinite; therefore, *Spirit is all*. 'There is no matter' is not only the axiom of true Christian Science, but it is the only basis upon which this Science can be demonstrated." (*Miscellany*) Elsewhere she says, "So long as matter is the basis of practice, illness cannot be efficaciously treated by the metaphysical process." (*Science and Health*)

The history of reformatory movements shows that the radicalism of today becomes the conservatism of tomorrow. Look what happened to primitive Christianity when it became the state church of Rome. The magnificent healings which had followed the ascension ceased, and the spiritual vacuum and gross materialism of the dark ages followed. Compromises such as this have repeatedly set back the clock of human progress. Today the tendency to mix matter and Spirit threatens the very Cause of Christian Science. But our Leader takes a clear-cut stand when she says, "It is not wise to take a halting and half-way position or to expect to work equally with Spirit and matter, Truth and error. There is but one way — namely, God and His idea — which leads to spiritual being. The scientific government of the body must be attained through the divine Mind. It is impossible to gain control over the body in any other way. On this fundamental point, timid conservatism is absolutely inadmissible. Only through radical reliance on Truth can scientific healing power be realized." (*Science and Health*) Again, she advises us, "Teach the dangerous possibility of dwarfing the spiritual understanding and demonstration of Truth by sin, or by recourse to material means for healing. Teach the meekness and might of life 'hid with Christ in God,' and there will be no desire for other healing methods. You render the divine law of healing obscure and void, when you weigh the human in the scale with the divine, or limit in any direction of thought the omnipresence and omnipotence of God." (ibid)

Most Christian Scientists genuinely endeavor to at least refrain from actually using physical remedies. But so often our healings are delayed because of a secretly-held mental reservation that says, for example, "Oh I wouldn't take any drugs because I'm a good little Christian Scientist; but if I did, they would probably heal me!" We become Christian Science martyrs, refusing even the theory — and understanding why. *And understanding why!* One suggestion that I might make in order to aid this effort is that you read the chapter 'Physiology' in the textbook, and read it with this question in mind: "Why don't I use material remedies?"

At one time in Sunday School, one of the teachers read to her class a beautiful testimony from *The Christian Science Journal* relating a healing of a young boy who was bitten by a snake. Realizing what had happened, he took no human steps, but he sat quietly and prayed. She asked her class of twelve-year olds what they thought of the wonderful way in which he had dealt with this. To her amazement, every child in the class said the boy's response had been dumb; that he should have sucked the poison out of the wound. They were so conditioned by community standards and education to seek a material remedy as normal that it seemed downright stupid and maybe unnecessary to rely on God in a situation such as this.

Now, stop and think for a moment. If you're faced with this problem, honest injun, what remedy would seem natural to you — particularly those of you who have been Boy Scouts or Girl Scouts, or who have had wilderness training? Do you see how mentally pervasive such material suggestions may be? This can be a little reminder how very important the continuing education and developing of our spiritual sense are to all of us. We cannot rely on both Spirit and matter or dwell in a divided mental house.

In *The Christian Science Journal* of November 1957 there is a statement from the then Board of Directors, entitled "The Christian Science Standard of Healing." It says in part:

> If one has failed to experience healing through Christian Science treatment and is tempted to resort to material means, the reason the healing has not been effected is often that the patient has been entertaining the subtle belief that material means can heal more effectively than Christian Science. It is such wrong thinking that, if not corrected, may ultimately lead him to resort to material means.
>
> Such mental reservations indicate that the student must completely give up the theory of *materia medica* and not merely give up its remedies. In order to be completely free from *materia medica*, one must reject its theory and opinions as to the origin, name, nature, symptoms, and effects of disease and must recognize that disease is never a material condition, but is a false mental state which is healed only by the Christ, Truth.

This is the radicalism of Christian Science. It is a radicalism of conviction and understanding, not simply one of abstinence. In our efforts to gain an understanding, to acquaint ourselves with the spiritual facts, we must keep our spiritual models fresh and uppermost in thought. Perhaps a little illustration will highlight the importance of this work.

Suppose some morning you received a call from a trusted friend telling you of the presence in your area of a fraudulent gold mine salesman. Your friend warns you rather specifically of the methods. Well, that afternoon there's a knock at your door and there he is, Mr. Suede Shoes, himself — a gold mine stock salesman, par excellence! He greets you very nicely and begins to present the details of his wonderful investment opportunity. What a picture he paints!

Now, in all likelihood, in spite of all his "evidence," you won't even allow him into your house, but would stop him at the door. But if by one means or another he does get in, the warnings of your friend will still ring clearly in your ears, enabling you to meet each of his arguments or "proofs," no matter how convincing they appear, with an instant refutation, silently or audibly. Why? Because in being forewarned, you have been forearmed!

Now, what if it has been several months since you received the phone call from your friend and Mr. Suede Shoes knocks at your door? You have allowed the warning to grow dim and indistinct in your thought. Will you be as alert? I doubt it! This is why Mrs. Eddy says that *daily study* is the *duty* of Christian Scientists, so that we shall remain aware of the spiritual facts which alert us to the blandishments of materiality. It behooves us to spend time in our closet of prayer, communing with our trusted Father, keeping our models clear and bright.

Haven't we all seen instances where people have turned to medical means for healing and as a result appear to express a better sense of health? Clearly, these are not expressions of God's doing or a progress Spiritward. Are not they more like the math student who, rather than working out the problems given in his textbook and gaining an understanding of the mathematical principles involved, has deviously turned to the back of the book and copied his answers? His paperwork may look as correct as the student's who struggled, worked out the problem and came to the same answer. But has the shortcut profited him anything at all in the way of understanding, growth, progress, or confidence?

Won't this lack of understanding at some point in his experience inevitably limit his progress and his accomplishments? What if there is no list in the back of the book the next time there's a problem to solve — or no medical aid available? But when the healing has been accomplished through prayer, the understanding and confidence that has been gained brings a freedom from fear and a confidence in God that no material effort could ever bring.

The goal is not simply to attain physical health or material wealth, the perfect companion or career — the world's "right" answers; but to gain in spiritual understanding, confidence in Truth, and dominion. The right answers — healings — will accompany this understanding as surely as they do in mathematics. But they are only a sign of the deeper, invisible things which have been gained through our struggles, and struggles there may be, but there is no shortcut nor alternative. Jonah's uncomfortable trip in the whale to Nineveh demonstrates that, doesn't it?

This radical reliance is well illustrated in a testimony printed in the October 13, 1956 *Christian Science Sentinel*. It tells of a little five-year old boy who ". . . had the middle finger of his left hand severed just above the second joint. According to material laws, the child would be maimed all his life." But the family turned unreservedly, radically, to Christian Science. The testimony goes on to say, "At no time in the entire experience did the child suffer pain. Within a month the hand was completely normal. The so-called flesh, bone, joint, nail — all the elements that were needed grew again, and the demonstration was complete." It goes on to cover in considerable detail the treatments given.

Mrs. Eddy tells us, "We must silence this lie of material sense with the truth of spiritual sense." (*Science and Health*) Let's look at this spiritual sense that she speaks of continually in her writing. She tells us that we must "mentally educate and develop the spiritual sense or perceptive faculty by which one learns the metaphysical treatment of disease." (*Christian Healing*)

Who has this spiritual sense? We all have it, whether we know it or not, whether we admit it or not. For instance with which of the so-called physical senses do we trust? Could you describe trust in terms of color, shape, size, texture or weight? Could you learn of it by using a microscope? You would be hard pressed to create or destroy trust materially, would you not? Of course, the same is true of joy, tenderness, harmony, honesty, contentment, forgiveness, compassion and freedom, but you are thoroughly convinced of their existence, aren't you? Only through spiritual sense do you know these; only through spiritual sense have you experienced these. Don't they constitute all, absolutely all, that is worthwhile and sought after in our lives? Why, our lives would become veritably unlivable without them. The very laws that we depend on are only mental concepts.

The statute books and the road signs are just hieroglyphics or symbols that refer to laws — all mental concepts. If the capitol of the state were involved in a huge earthquake and all of the statute books fell into a big void, would that affect the laws for a moment? It's all mental. We live in a mental world. We're depending upon mental things. When we talk about spiritual sense, that's what we are talking about.

Of course, mortal mind tries consistently to convince us that it is something material that we seek, that a particular object or a state of physical well-being or another person's presence will bring us satisfaction. But we see so much evidence that they don't, that wealth, or fame, or people, or even physical health, do not of themselves bring contentment. Contrariwise, we often see true peace and satisfaction in places where the physical accouterments of wealth, fame, power, and persons are not present. How often have we seen dedicated teachers, remote church preachers, nurses, writers or artists, totally devoted to their work, absolutely content in what they are doing, for a purpose not material? We learn from this that physical sense is a counterfeit, and that only spiritual sense enables us to behold the real, the genuine, the lasting, the satisfying, that which has real substance.

Once we come to see the actuality, presence, practicality and value of spiritual sense, we will educate it and develop it. We will find ourselves more willing to turn away from the reports of physical sense and toward the facts of Spirit.

A wise man was once told that the value of anything was almost indeterminable because there are so many variables involved. "Nonsense," he replied, "the formula is simple: just what will you give up for it?" Try this and you will soon know how valuable something is to you. *What will you give up for it?*

What are we willing to give up for spiritual growth? Isn't this one of the primary self-serving cautions of mortal mind? Mortal mind argues that this is our day in the sun, live it up! Later perhaps, when I get a little more gray hair, then I'm going to do it. But in turning from mortality to spirituality, do we actually give up a single desirable, comforting, fulfilling, satisfying thing? Not one.

It is something like a little boy who came to show his dad his latest find — a wiggly, deadly scorpion, clutched in his little fist. "Put it down, son," cried the father. "No Daddy, it's mine." "Please throw it down, son," the father pleaded. "But I want to keep it Daddy," the boy protested. Then his father had the presence of mind to suggest, "Put it down, honey, and I'll give you some candy." Well, the child immediately complied. We don't readily give up something until we have a better replacement. That's true with all of us. The more we come to know spiritual sense, to feel its influence on our thoughts and lives, the more willing we are to turn from the physical sense testimony.

Haven't you noticed that mankind doesn't usually let go of

something until it can be replaced with something of greater value? A taste of the fruits of Spirit brings a willingness to take the next step and reject reports of the physical senses or false images of thought, even in the face of a lifetime of spurious education and acceptance. For a cave that has been dark for centuries is illumined instantly with the first beams of light.

This turning from the physical senses is a task. We've been taught all our lives that that is how we get a glimpse of reality. They are the windows to reality, we learn all our lives — those five senses. But as a matter of fact, they are total illusions. The only way we really know is through spiritual sense. There is no other source of reality. I would like to share an experience with you which illustrates what happens when we agree to turn radically from the physical picture to the reports of spiritual sense.

Several years ago I was serving as Christian Science chaplain at San Quentin prison. A young man who had attended our services a few times anxiously greeted me one day as I entered the gate. He was extremely agitated and thrust a medical report into my hands. He said, "Read this!" The medical report stated that all his tests and lab reports proved him to be severely diabetic and suggested that medication was necessary immediately. This man said that the doctor had told him that if he did not take this medication his condition would grow steadily worse, and he would die. He apparently had no alternative! He then put to me the $64 question: "Will Christian Science heal me?" I told him that there was nothing that Christian Science could not heal when its teachings were applied by an honest and trusting heart. He asked if I would help him. I assured him that I would be happy to help, and reminded him that although the decision was his, we didn't give Christian Science treatment to anyone who was having medical treatment. I endeavored to explain why. He was quiet for a few moments, and then he said, "OK. Let's go. What do I do?"

My first request was that he refrain from examining, diagnosing, judging or conjecturing about his body — audibly or silently.

He was simply to feed it, sleep it, bathe it, dress it and forget it! Why? Because it had nothing to do with the problem, absolutely nothing! It was a red herring which would divert his attention. Thought and thought alone was all we were concerned with, so a rejection of all sense reports (even if in written form) was absolutely necessary. Perhaps most importantly, I told him of some of the circumstances surrounding the writing of *Science and Health*, and urged him to accept it as revelation! He borrowed a copy, and I gave him some citations to read and pray over. He grasped that book as though it was his very link to life, and in a very practical way it was!

Now, I might tell you that until the following week when we were able to have our next visit, I had another patient to deal with regarding this problem — ME!

That doctor's report was so explicit, and my friend's physical condition so alarming that a false sense of responsibility tried repeatedly to enter thought. It argued that this courageous young man had placed his life on the line — literally! Each time the words of that report came to mind, the physical sense picture had to be mentally rejected and spiritual sense's picture of man accepted. As the reports of spiritual sense replaced the lie of physicality, a beautiful picture of man's present perfection was revealed to my consciousness. This correct view adhered to, rejoiced in, and glorified in with singleness of mind and deep gratitude, brought a change in thinking and the side-effect of healing.

When I came through the gate next week, there he was waiting. Now, not that I was anxious you understand, but I must say that I was surely happy to see him standing there with a big grin on his face. He thrust another medical report into my hand and said, "Just read that one." It reported that all signs of diabetes were negative, and verified his perfect state of health. He told me that the doctors had kept him for hours, retesting and reexamining him. They couldn't understand it because the very recent diabetic indications had been so pronounced. He proudly held up his medicine bottle and told me that he had not touched it! The reward of radical reliance has always been a heartening one when claims of incurability, accompanied by alarming appearances, have been suggested to thought.

The handling of fear is of paramount importance in our efforts to be radical Christian Scientists. Every one of us knows that, and particularly when there has been some suggestion to thought that it is serious and that it hurts, or it may even be held out as something fatal. I don't think there is anyone that has not been touched with this thing of fear, and this fear is what brings about compromise. So, we can't be afraid to be afraid.

As this is such a common struggle, let me tell you how one practitioner handled it. Her infant son was very ill and running a high fever. She became so alarmed at the symptoms (the physical sense reports) that she called another practitioner to come over and help her. When she arrived and saw the situation she said, "Well, all that must be dealt with here is fear." The mother told me, "That did not help much. I didn't have to have a practitioner come over just to tell me I was scared. I knew that already. So I sent her home as soon as I could and then I literally went down on my knees in prayer, in simple reliance on God. Just then, the words came to me from *Science and Health*: 'Fear never stopped being and it's action.' I realized — why I can be just as afraid as I can be, and it's not going to stop the Christ. You know what that did to the fear!" The fever disappeared in short order, and when the child awoke, he was perfectly well. She said, "I learned from this experience that all fear can do is make you sweat a little, but it can't stop the Christ in its healing action." Fear can be faced and dealt with, and the material sense testimony put to one side as we stand radically for the facts of Spirit.

"Fear never stopped being and its action." Isn't it wonderful what a single truth from our textbook can accomplish? May I take a moment to dwell on the importance of the statements of truth contained in our treasured textbook? Remember, this book is like no other. Truly, it is revelation. In all other sources of knowledge, we are encouraged to question, question, question. It says that man came out of the swamp and went to the moon by questioning. That doesn't create any problems for me now of questioning any book but this book. I've had some people that were quite educated say, "How can you say that? How can you say this book, of all the books in the world, that you accept without a question?" The answer is simple, because it works, and I believe it with all my heart, and I could talk here for an hour on incidents that have brought this conviction, that these are by revelation. Mrs. Eddy used to just clap her hands together, and she'd say to members of her household, "Just listen to this. Listen to this." She'd be so excited about something. About three weeks before she went on she said, "I am just now beginning to understand this book." It's true, this is a book of revelation, and the more humbly and certainly we accept its statements, the better work we accomplish because it goes to the very crux of it, without a question. This practitioner saw this statement — fear about fear — and it ended it for her immediately.

Mrs. Eddy tells us that, "Sleep and mesmerism explain the mythical nature of material sense." (*Science and Health*) She uses these illustrations often, perhaps because the sense reports are actually a part of our waking dream which she refers to throughout her writings. "Mortal existence is a dream; mortal existence has no real entity," she tells us in this book. Then she asks, "Is there any more reality in the waking dream of mortal existence than in a sleeping dream? There cannot be . . . " We can consider this analogy prayerfully when we are tempted to "stand aghast" at sense pictures.

Suppose some loved one is having a frightening dream, a nightmare. He's crying out that a tiger is chasing him and he's trying to run away from it. You would try to awaken him because you would like him to have a pleasant dream, or better yet, to wake up. But suppose you were unable to awaken him, and for some reason you must leave. You can do so without great concern because you know that presently he will awake and there won't be a tooth or claw mark on him! Well, even so in this waking dream, and the fearful sense pictures that we encounter with it. Based on what Mrs. Eddy tells us, they are no more real than the tiger in the sleeping dream and leave not a single mark on man, the real man, the one beheld in spiritual sense as immortal — that is, birthless, deathless, perfect, indestructible, harmonious, functioning, alive. Now that's the real man. Milton Simon put it this way, "The belief that five and four are ten cannot be put into intelligent consciousness. Just so, any difficulty with what is termed the body is not in body, but is a belief of something untrue that never touches God's man. This is strikingly illustrated when one considers that a dream never becomes part of one's body. If you dream you are in pain, only while you dream will you feel pain. Your body remains unharmed. Awakening from the dream, you see that there is no pain to destroy." (*The Christian Science Journal*, September 1948, "All is Mind and Its Ideas")

Mrs. Eddy required members of her household, when they were working on a problem, to put two words in front of the problem — *belief of*. That headache was a belief of a headache. Now why was this so important? Can you think of any other two words that make the transposition any more immediate? It's a dream — it's not a reality. If we see it this way, we deal with it altogether differently because we're getting rid of a belief only, we're not doing anything to a body. There's not an ounce of matter in a body; it's all an illusion. That's why Mrs. Eddy said that through sleep and mesmerism we're able to see this. As we turn more and more to the spiritual sense, we, too, will see that there's nothing to fix about a body.

Now let's briefly review some of the factors we've covered concerning our desire to be more radical Christian Scientists.

1. We turn away from the theory of *materia medica* as well as from diagnosis of any kind. I don't care what kind of re-

ports they are, how many x-rays, how many pathology reports, it is absolutely pointless. They are not true. For when we diagnose, aren't we looking for a cause in matter in order that we might account for an effect in matter, a symptom which the senses have reported? We must be equally diligent in refusing to search for psychological causes in regard to personal, economic or business problems, for these are just as pernicious to our effort to side with Spirit, Mind's allness, as the other.

2. We've seen how shallow is the materialist's contention that anything real must be cognizable by the physical sense. We'll continue to see this as we become increasingly aware of the substance of what spiritual sense reports. It is through spiritual sense that we know and find a lasting sense of joy, inspiration, peace, comfort, happiness, trust, honesty, courage, beauty, tenderness, love, integrity, health and satisfaction — only through spiritual sense.

3. We've talked of how turning from physical sense testimony to the evidence seen through spiritual sense brings healing. Even when the reports are as alarming as they were to me following the reading of that diagnosis of the prisoner with diabetes.

4. We have touched on how we might deal with fear, relying on the truth of Mrs. Eddy's statement that "Fear never stopped being and its action." A mother dealt with and overcame the belief of fear showing itself as fever. As we accept the truth of this statement, we will find ourselves better able to resist with authority the appearance of the sense reports, and that's all they are, appearances, not reality. We don't cry at the movie or agonize over the dream; we come to understand its illusory nature.

5. These are waking dreams, as Mrs. Eddy refers to them, and have no more substance than our sleeping dreams. Think of this for a moment. Our Leader has directed our thought to some-

thing we've all known and experienced — a dream. We've all laughed, cried, agonized, feared, and rejoiced, or wanted to go back and get kissed again in the context of a dream. We've all awakened to find that the cause of these feelings was an illusion. Even so, this waking dream is but an illusion from which we awaken as we glimpse the reality and presence of Spirit.

Our radicalism must be found in Spirit. It shall lead us unmistakably to what our human stand in certain situations must be, and we will take it! Mrs. Eddy in her address to the National Convention in Chicago said, "Men and women of the nineteenth century, are you called to voice a higher order of Science? Then obey this call. Go if you must, to the dungeon or the scaffold, but take not back the words of Truth. How many are there ready to suffer for a righteous cause, to stand a long siege, take the front rank, face the foe, and be in the battle every day?" (*Miscellaneous Writings*)

I remember catching an inspiring glimpse of this spirit while talking with one of our early workers in the movement. A little white-haired lady not even five feet tall, but a Goliath in conviction, told about some of the early days of Christian Science in England. It wasn't easy there in the very stronghold of conservative religion and the glorification of materialism, but those dauntless followers of this radical "healing cult" (as they were known) stood. She said that in treating children, particularly, it was hazardous, because it was illegal. "But," she said, "we went forth," (and quoting Mrs. Eddy) "prepared 'to go to the dungeon or the scaffold' if needs be." Then she threw back her head and laughed with such joy and confidence. "But we didn't have to, because we healed them," she said. It wasn't an exercise of will power or fanaticism. It was the demonstration of Spirit understood, and that's spiritual radicalism!

It's what we must see with our children. I know how difficult it is in the circumstances of these adverse reports, and the appearances, and the fear now about the legal, but if we will stand

and look through the spiritual sense we're going to see more healings. I've just seen healing after healing of children's cases when it looked so bad — even broken arms and legs, healed without even being set. It's when we turn radically to it. You're not fixing matter in any way.

Is there anyone who does not know in his own affairs which of two possible steps presented is the more nearly right? Are we using what we do have and what we do know and taking the step that we do see? Our Leader once said that, "God never leaves us without light enough to take one step. Do not quit walking until the light gives out." Look around, isn't there light enough to take one forward step. We may not see the whole solution to the problem, but we have enough light to take our next step. And that's all we need, for Jesus counseled, "Take no thought for the morrow," knowing that today's obedience will make way for tomorrow.

Christian Science is a radical religion. It's not an easy religion. No one ever said that it was, but it's rewards more than outweigh the effort we put into it!

DAILY IDENTIFICATION

I would like to discuss with you the need for "daily identification." A Christian Scientist was riding home from work one day when a neighbor he was riding with suddenly asked him a very direct question. "Tell me, what do you think of yourself?"

"Oh," he said, "I don't think you really want to know." But the neighbor assured him that he did, so he answered, "Well, I think I am in reality man, the image and likeness of God, His perfect child, and so are you by the same token."

His neighbor then told him that he had heard that Christian Scientists so believed, but he was interested in seeing how consistent they were about applying it in their daily lives — just how deep their convictions went. And he went on to say that he very much appreciated his including the statement, ". . . and so are you by the same token." His applying this truth to all men indicated the deep Christianity of Christian Science.

This answer to his neighbor caused the Christian Scientist to reconsider the depth and consistency of his own daily identification of himself as the image and likeness of God. He began to ask himself daily, "What do I really think of myself? Am I really thinking of man as the image and likeness of God?" He said that in considering this, he discovered a number of mortal concepts and human opinions that very much needed to be eliminated if he were to be really consistent. For instance, there was a growth that was growing larger on his face all the time. He realized that if he was consistent in his knowledge of man's perfection, it would not be there. Certainly, God, the Giver of all good, had not caused this imperfection. He realized that he had been believing in the reality of matter. *He had been believing in the reality of matter.* And when he turned humbly to God, it was revealed to him that because he had been thinking in terms of mortal imperfection in himself and others, there seemed to be a blemish on his face. He began right then to establish that man is always spiritual and perfect — that right where man is, and everywhere, divine Spirit is making itself manifest in all its spiritual perfection, for man is this spiritual manifestation.

Now, that's not very complicated, is it? It certainly isn't in theory. Sometimes, practicing it is a little more difficult. When the first day he started practicing seeing everyone as spiritually perfect, that night he had a dream. He dreamt that an elephant trunk was growing on the end of his nose. The dream seemed so real that when he woke up, he found himself pulling on the end of his nose to see if that trunk was still there. "But why doesn't a trunk grow on my nose?" he asked himself. "Because it isn't natural," he reasoned. Because he wasn't an elephant.

So it was just as unnatural for a false material sense of growth to appear on his body, because he wasn't material. Just as he wasn't an elephant, he wasn't material. God doesn't cause such a growth in man. It was just a mortal dream, no more natural and real than the elephant trunk had been. So every time he was tempted to check up on the growth, he turned his thought away from the material sense testimony to the thought of that elephant's trunk. He realized that he wouldn't be checking on the trunk to see if it was there, because he knew it was never really there.

This seems a little hard to conceive of sometimes when our five senses are saying emphatically to us that we are made of matter. He knew there simply was no imperfection in God's one and only spiritual universe. One day, he noticed that the blemish was gone. There was no more growth. He simply had consistently identified himself as the perfect likeness of a perfect God, instead of an imperfect mortal. He saw there had never been an imperfect man to be healed, only a lie about a perfect one to be destroyed. You see, he saw he was not in the body repair business. He was in the lie destruction business. Not for a moment did he start out to repair a body. That's the red herring that mortal mind drags across our path. He started out single-mindedly with one purpose, and that was to destroy a lie, and the method was so simple — that of identifying himself properly.

Nathan Talbot makes this correct premise for healing so clear in a recent *Christian Science Sentinel* article entitled, "After the Healing, What to Notice." He writes, "If we start from the basis that God has already made man perfect, the healing will be more a matter of spiritual awakening, the discovery and admission of divine harmony. If this is the way we prayed, than what are we most likely to notice after the healing? We will see evidence of real spiritual existence. We will recognize some measure of moral and spiritual progress in our lives. Writing of the advantages of healing and endless spiritual progress through prayer, Mrs. Eddy explains that a person healed by Christian Science is not only healed of his disease, but he has advanced morally and spiritually."

We had an interesting testimony at our church a few weeks ago. A woman gave a testimony about how she was preparing some vegetables, and she sliced the end of her finger off. She told how she just put it back on and put a Band-Aid around it, and then she talked about how she thought, how she identified herself as a spiritual idea, and she went through that whole process with such joy of recollection of what she had learned in that process, and then she sat down. And you know we are so used to looking to see, "Now, what's the effect of that healing." It was like she had dropped one shoe and hadn't finished dropping the other yet. About twenty minutes later, she got up and said, "Oh yes, I forgot to tell you — it grew back so perfectly, I don't even remember which finger it was." It was so impressive to me that she had seen that the important thing was *not* the physical healing. The important thing was the spiritual development that she made in it.

Consider the benefits of the Christian Scientist's radical answer to the question his friend asked and the healing it bestowed on him. If we can ask ourselves this question every day, "Am I the image and likeness of God?" and then require of ourselves an answer — an answer which sets forth the spiritual reality of our identity — think what this truth will do for us and everyone whom our lives touch. It is a vital matter of our identification, isn't it?

Mortal mind tries to identify us by one or more of these three methods: physicality, personality, or intellect. You know how false and misleading these characteristics can be. For instance, let's suppose you could just step into a super-molecular transfer machine, right out of Star Wars. You could turn some dials and select your physical appearance — whether you are going to be tall or short, blue-eyed or brown-eyed, blonde or brunette, red-headed or bald-headed — just push a button and assume any appearance you wished, and you would be permanently changed. And the same thing goes for your personality or intellect — you could choose to be an Einstein or a Humphrey Bogart. Now, would your true identity be altered one single bit? Of course not. So we see that these material factors do not identify man. Man can only be correctly identified spiritually — as God's likeness.

Now, what about health appearances as identification? Can you do much about that? "He looks like warmed-over death," or "He looks the picture of health," or something in between. It often actually includes a kind of unconsciousness diagnosis, doesn't it? And it's always based on the claim of dualism — Spirit and matter. Isn't that the big thing we meet? Isn't that what the world thinks — there is a spirit living within this house of matter? We take a very radical stand when we turn away from this. Whenever we get on the side of matter-identification, we take away from the side of Spirit.

True identification is the very reverse of it. As our Leader puts it, "Obedience to material law prevents full obedience to spiritual law." *"Obedience to material law prevents full obedience to spiritual law."* Correct identification never involves Spirit and matter. The spiritual is the actual, always present whether we know it or not, or whether we see it or not, for the physical appearance

— that waking and dreaming illusion — does not indicate a second existence.

There are not two existences. Spirit is the actual and only existence, and matter is simply the waking, dreaming illusion — the unreality of existence. It truly has only the substance of a waking dream. And when we awaken from it, every ungodlike quality vanishes, leaving revealed the Godlike qualities.

Now, how does the establishing in consciousness of the ideal real man — God's image and likeness — affect our relationship with others? Well, you remember the last line of our daily prayer, "And may Thy word enrich the affections of all mankind, and govern them." That is from the *Church Manual*.

It's not enough, we come to see, to claim this idea for ourselves, but we must claim it as well for all mankind. That's one of the rules. Remember, we live by rules in Christian Science, and that's one of the rules — that we claim it for all mankind. We can't avoid it.

A young soldier was serving in the armed services, and he was having a terrible time with the brutal sergeant he was under, who was making his life absolutely miserable. Finally, in desperation, the young man sought the help of a Christian Science practitioner. After relating the circumstances to the practitioner and telling in detail how he was praying, it became evident to the practitioner why the young soldier's prayers were not effective. He had been trying to see a mortal as God's spiritual idea, whereas he needed to see God's spiritual idea *instead* of a mortal. He had been trying to see the sergeant as the image and likeness of God, whereas he needed to see the image and likeness of God *instead* of the sergeant. He had been trying to change a bad mortal into a good mortal, whereas he needed to change his own thought from believing that identity is mortal — good or bad. He had been believing that he was a mortal among mortals, being abused by another mortal; whereas he needed to realize that he was a spiritual idea among spiritual ideas, and in the presence of Spirit and the atmosphere of divine Love, under the command of God, the only Mind there is. He had been trying to love a mortal, which is not man; whereas he needed to love God's completely spiritual idea, which is man. He had been trying to eliminate discordant mortality, whereas he needed to eliminate the belief there is any mortality, discordant or otherwise. As he did, the relationship became more harmonious.

Now, true prayer is not praying for God's allness to heal a material situation. It never is. It is the humble acceptance of Spirit's perfect allness and man's completely perfect spiritual identity, instead of the material situation. The tendency, all too often, is to pray for material results. But the effectual prayer is the acknowledgment of God's ever-present allness and perfection. Because of the importance of this concept, may I further illustrate how the establishment of this spiritual, ideal, invisible man in thought has healed?

A man working for a large organization found himself embroiled in what the world would classify a clash of personalities with his department head, whom he thought disliked him and wanted very much to see him fired, although the Christian Scientist tried in every way to be kind and helpful, a good red-blooded American boy, for America, motherhood, apple pie. In spite of all the good things he tried to do, every effort was rebuffed. He worried about the situation until the day rheumatism crippled him. When a practitioner was called, he asked the man a series of questions. First, he asked whether he loved everyone. Now, any Christian Scientist knows how you are supposed to answer that one. Then the practitioner asked whether everyone loved him. Well, this necessarily brought out the problem with his supervisor. The practitioner then asked what God was.

"Well, God is Love," he replied, almost automatically.

"Where is God?" was the next question.

"God is ever-present," he answered.

"Do you believe these two statements are true?" asked the practitioner.

"Well, yes I do," said the patient.

"Then tell me, how do you reconcile those two statements with the one you just made — that out there in the consciousness of someone is a thing called hatred?"

The man saw that in order to be consistent, he had to see divine Love as ever-present, manifested as God's man, not only in his experience, but in the experience of everyone. Up until that moment, he knew that it was important for him to love others, but what of their feeling about him? Well, he always regarded that as more or less *their* business.

Now, for the very first time, he saw that it was very much *his* business. What *he* thought about what *they* thought is what had to be healed. Now mind you, he didn't have to go out and change the thinking of somebody out there. It was *what he thought about what they thought* — all within his own consciousness — that had to be dealt with. It was part of his daily identification and acknowledgment of only one Mind. That's one of the rules. You can't do it without applying the rules

He began to rejoice in the words of the daily prayer, trusting that divine Love is truly enriching the affections of all mankind and governing them. He began to see man as the image and likeness of divine Love, instead of a mortal, hating or hated. And, oh yes, the interesting side effect of this thinking was that the rheumatism disappeared promptly and there was a reconciliation with the department head.

I almost hesitate to tell you the results now, because the important thing is not the healing; the important thing was the changing of his consciousness. I would urge you to be thinking more in that line of not working to change matter, but to change our state of consciousness. The healing is the side effect — it's irresistible because it is all in consciousness. There isn't any matter to be diseased. There isn't any matter — good or bad matter.

Mrs. Eddy says this in *Miscellany.* First, she tells us what we are, because we know we exist. To say to somebody all of a sudden, "Well, you don't have a body, you aren't there and you have no matter" — that's a pretty big one to swallow, because you know you *do* exist. First she says, "*All is Spirit*," and adds, "'There is no matter' is not only the axiom of true Christian Science; it is the only basis upon which this Science can be demonstrated." That says it, and we have to practice that way. That's one of the rules.

Spiritual man *is*; sinning, struggling mortal man is only the waking human illusion or mistaken sense of God's perfect spiritual man. In *Retrospection and Introspection* Mrs. Eddy speaks so plainly of this. She says, "The great difference between these opposites is that the human material concept is unreal, and the divine concept or idea is spiritually real. One is false while the other is true."

Spiritual man — the only substance really at hand — does not need healing. Why? Because man is God's very likeness. A waking dream, like a mirage, is non-existent, and we simply cannot do anything to that which does not exist. The dream has no substance. This deflection, which we call mortal man, can and often does include illusions called disease, discord, fear, and poverty. But this deflection, too, is just as untrue, a false image. In *Miscellaneous Writings* Mrs. Eddy tell us, " . . . man is incapable of originating; nothing can be formed apart from God, good, the all-knowing Mind."

When we mistakenly identify ourselves as material, and then set about, by one means or another, to heal a physical body, what are we doing? Well, it's as though you are going on a railroad trip. When you go down to the station, a lot of your friends are there to see you off, and one of them went down on the tracks and, all of a sudden, in genuine alarm, he said, "Well, you can't take that train! Look, those tracks go together right outside of town." And all of you look, and sure enough, they do.

At that point, you have three options. You can pick up your bag and go home, because any fool wouldn't get on a train where the tracks are going to go together; or you could learn the facts about this, that those tracks are parallel. So with a conviction and trust that the tracks do not merge, you will get on the train and go your way. Now, besides those two choices, you have a third option. You can all go down on the tracks, hold a prayer meeting, and give the tracks a treatment and try to heal them!

Obviously you can't heal an illusion. The tracks, in fact, did not need to be healed — were they not perfect all the time? What needed to be healed? The tracks? No, only a mistaken view of the tracks. So, ultimately, we come to identify the unseen or invisible tracks as real, and we refuse to give substance or reality to the physical sense testimony of converging tracks, or to try and heal them. So we see that we could deal calmly with the unseen or invisible tracks with no trouble, couldn't we?

Now, is there any Christian Scientist who does not accept that they are, individually, the image and likeness of God — an invisible God? Are we in agreement on that? Then let us go to what Mrs. Eddy says so clearly in the first section of the Christian Science platform regarding the invisible man. Remember what she says? "Eye hath neither seen God nor His image and likeness. Neither God nor the perfect man can be discerned by the material senses." Now, can you identify yourself without reference to your physical body? Think of it for a moment. Can you? When we start to consider ourselves in this way, it makes us pause and think, doesn't it? No matter how many times we may have blithely mouthed the words, I am the image and likeness of God, and most of us have, somehow we still envision a dual presence that can be discerned physically — maybe a good kind of physical presence, but still, at least in part, physical. So to come right out and say that the real man is absolutely invisible brings us up rather short, doesn't it? Most of us feel something like the little girl whose father was putting her to bed one night, and when they walked into the dark bedroom, he felt those little arms tighten around his neck, and she said, "I'm afraid, Daddy."

And he said, "Well, God's in here with you, honey, just the same."

And she says, "Yes, I know Daddy, but I'd like to have somebody with skin around them!"

Aren't we pretty much this way in our identification? Yet the God we speak of is invisible, for John said, "No man hath seen God at any time." And Jesus confirmed this in declaring, "He hath neither heard His voice at any time, nor seen His shape." Paul speaks of the image of the invisible God. So, if God is invisible — and He is — then His image and likeness must be invisible. Actually thinking of man as invisible puts us in a whole new ballgame. See what it does to disease? No one ever thinks of a disease except in connection with a visible, material body, do they? And the same thing with sin, and age, and lack, and the like. They just can't continue when man is seen as spiritual and invisible. It seems to make it easier to see through claims of mortal mind when there is no material body for them to inhabit or affect. We can more easily see man as immune, untouched by mortal mind's claims, indestructible and eternal.

Now we realize that with our dear ones, it isn't anything physical that we love. Yet we know them so well. In fact, the dearer they are, the less we are aware of their bodies. Isn't that so? The more we are aware of and value their spiritual qualities, the spiritual unseen and invisible man, the less their physical appearances mean to us. And we can begin to see that the individual we identify is truly invisible to the physical senses. Now, that's a fact. And the sooner we begin to think of ourselves that way, the more effective our work will be. If we describe them, it wouldn't be physically, but in non-material terms — honest, trusting, loving, tender, patient, kind, and the like. Only with strangers that we don't know, do we perhaps revert to physical description.

The last few weeks, I have had occasion to write several letters of recommendation for people. Why, I don't know, but as I wrote them, the thought came to me about these letters I had written. Not in one letter did I describe them physically. Every quality that those employers were thinking about, was non-physical. That's the man that we really value. Now somebody that is making an application to pull a plow, I might give some thought as to whether he had muscles or how much he weighed. But even in that case, wouldn't you be thinking, "How well do they work with others? How obedient are they? How faithful are they?" Isn't that the kind of things you would think about, even if it looked like they were going to deal in a physical activity?

Everyone looks for these things, but we don't call it that. We can begin then by realizing that the perfect man, or spiritual ideal, with whom we seek to identify, is actually invisible. And that tends to put us back on the track rather quickly when we're tempted with the idols of beautiful, desirable, glamorous appearing matter, or frightening appearing matter.

When the duality of an appealing picture of matter and Spirit is presented by mortal mind as a model, we can reject it through this simple test. Is it discernible in any way to the physical senses? When we begin to identify ourselves and others as this spiritual man, we proportionately divorce ourselves from the physical. Stop and think. With which part of your body, physical that is, do you originate, demonstrate, or even know that there are such things as honesty, love, peace, contentment, or any other quality or attribute of God. When with our physical senses can we report this? Obviously, every single thing that makes our lives worthwhile is a mental state that is discernible entirely through spiritual sense — totally invisible to the physical sense.

You remember that Mrs. Eddy tells us — that you must first mentally educate and develop the spiritual sense or perceptive faculty, and that's what we are in the job of doing now. We can see why this is of such importance, as it is through this sense alone that we can perceive or behold the spiritual man — the image and likeness of God that we all seek to know. The more this spiritual sense is developed, the clearer becomes this ideal generic man to us. Let's be acutely aware of what is taking place.

This awareness will cause us to consciously trust more unquestioningly this spiritual sense and its picture of man. The fact that man is invisible will cause us no problem, because in spiritual awareness, no reliance is placed on the material senses at all. The spiritual viewing can become to us as it did to Jesus, the normal, acceptable, substantial view of man, and our identification with it will become closer, more absolute, more trusted, and immediate. As our identification of the person shifts to these qualities, and to the activity of God's image and likeness, we are proportionately less impressed with the material, and our expectancy of healing increases. Like Moses, we endure by seeing Him who is invisible, for true expectancy is not expecting something to come to pass, but acknowledging everything to be what it is already, harmonious and spiritual. See how simple the concept is? It is the application of it that is difficult. Why? Because the physical senses put on such a show. It is completely illusion, but they do put on a show, and we have to learn not to cry at the movies!

Identifying yourselves and others as spiritual and invisible appears to be quite a step for us, doesn't it? But don't dismiss it as unattainable or unwanted. It's what Jesus, our Way-shower, talked and practiced. So we can start accepting this premise in our daily study and in small challenges. It comes "precept upon precept, line upon line," we are told, and in proportion as we are able to see it, our view is uplifted. Healings occur, and our lives change. You may ask yourself, "How long does a healing take?" Well, that all depends — if you are trying to change matter, that's a job that never ends. But, if you desire to reform consciousness with thoughts divine, it breaks all the barriers of time.

"EARTH'S PREPARATORY SCHOOL"

Let me begin by saying that we are all students — students in the school that Mrs. Eddy refers to as "earth's preparatory school." In thoughtfully considering this fact we necessarily begin with a heightened awareness of man's *immortality* as an idea of God. Our Leader, Mrs. Eddy, fully expected us to look upon and live our lives from this point of view — from this premise! In *Science and Health* she tells us: "Life is eternal. We should find this out, and begin the demonstration thereof."

Without an understanding or acceptance of our immortality, much of our discussion would be rather pointless and shallow; for her use of the word "preparatory" can only imply the preparation for an ultimate state of consciousness which knows only good — only true spirituality. Therefore we are, or should be, in the process of recognizing our present state of perfection; we should be gaining a consciousness of our present immortal life.

Though we have now but a small glimpse of our true selfhood as God's perfect man, and only "know in part" our perfection, we go forward, "precept upon precept," *expectantly*. It is an acceptance of the fact that we truly are eternal that makes this goal attainable. So let's agree that we are willing to consider everything discussed from the point of view that we are in fact deathless, eternal.

This discussion might very well be titled "An Exercise in Willingness," for underscoring everything we will be working with will be a sense of individual willingness. Why is this sense of willingness of such particular importance? Because everything relating to earth's preparatory school is based upon our willingness to accept Life as eternal and to live in a way that confirms this acceptance. Only from this basis will we be willing to accept the rules of earth's preparatory school as reasonable, and to study the spiritual facts carefully, and then see the daily problems and challenges we face not as curses, but simply as effective means of applying the facts of Science.

Mrs. Eddy's description of this life experience as a "school" is such an apt one, for no school accomplishes its work of education without demanding, on the part of the student, a willingness to obey its rules and apply them exactly. The disobedient and indifferent pupil makes little progress in any learning. Even so in earth's preparatory school! The intractable, unwilling student — those who are holding to material, temporal life as real — make little, if any, progress in understanding eternal Life. Such a reluctance to let go of materiality imprisons us in a material sense of life. Are we held in harsh bondage because of our unwillingness to let go of this false sense? In Exodus we read of Moses' wonderful willingness: "And the angel of the Lord appeared unto him in a flame of fire out of the midst of a bush: and he looked, and, behold, the bush burned with fire, and the bush was not consumed. And Moses said, I will now turn aside, and see this great sight, why the bush is not burnt. And when the Lord saw that he turned aside to see, God called unto him out of the bush . . . ."

It seems that the thing that prompted God to speak to Moses was the fact that Moses "turned aside to see." His point of view included a willingness to listen and to learn from his experiences.

Elizabeth Barrett Browning's poem catches the wonderful significance of this event: She writes:

Earth's crammed with heaven,
And every common bush afire with God.
And only he who sees takes off his shoes,
The rest sit round and pluck blackberries.

Isn't it true that earth, our human experience, has many heavenly signs, and bushes afire, furnishing us with inspiring learning opportunities? But there are few that "see" — that "turn aside" — take off their shoes, and learn the divine wisdom contained in everyday events. "The rest sit round and pluck blackberries."

"Earth's preparatory school," Mrs. Eddy terms it. What an interesting way of contemplating existence! A prep school! What a contrast to the world's view of life as finite and perilous "Eat, drink, and be merry: for tomorrow we die." And so necessarily, what a contrast in goals and purposes!

We can never forget that *our* goal, as practicing Christian Scientists, is to attain a *constant consciousness of the omnipotence and omnipresence of God.*

We must decide at which altar we will worship: matter or Spirit. If we do not deliberately seek spiritual growth and understanding, then by default the illusion of materiality becomes foremost in our experience. When we drift with the current of mortal mind's materialism, apparently making no choice, we have made a choice — *for no choice is a choice!* Let there be no doubt about this. By neglecting to make a deliberate choice to awaken through spiritual progress, we have elected to remain asleep in mortal mind's "waking dream." And it's no bargain!

A choice for Spirit, however, doesn't mean that there won't be challenges. There will be! Every one of our predecessors who made significant spiritual growth had challenges — often severe, demanding challenges. But they saw them as opportunities to grow, opportunities to advance, opportunities to draw closer to God, opportunities to prove His omnipotence for the sake of all mankind. Their problems weren't seen as stumbling-blocks, but as stepping-stones to a higher understanding of God! These spiritual leaders viewed life from the point of view of students in earth's preparatory school, and so were willing to build for eternity — to suffer and struggle, if need be, to work out the problem of being. They were humble students. They struggled, persevered, and used the problems to their advantage. And think how much more we know of reality because of their willingness to do so!

77

Though originally our purpose for studying Christian Science may have been to live more comfortable and materially productive lives, but our growth in understanding inevitably leads us to see more clearly the unlimited, eternal, spiritual nature of man. This realization then becomes our very purpose, and our inevitable enrollment in earth's preparatory school. To understand our true at-one-ment with God is what we now strive for. No goal, no study could possibly be of greater importance, of greater value

Every important spiritual step in human history has been preceded by the preparation of thought and heart, and by full-time attendance in earth's school. For instance, how willing was the army of Israel to stand up to the Philistine champion, Goliath, accepting as they had the power and invincibility of that giant? Can you blame them? Here was a trained, warrior, ten-and-a-half feet tall, whose armor alone weighed over one hundred and fifty pounds. Even the head of his iron spear weighed over twenty pounds. That might present a rather convincing image of material reality and power to anyone!

But David's years of prayer and spiritual education and problem-solving with his sheep had given him a confidence in the omnipotence of God. Had he not met the lion and the bear as material sense "problems"? And in solving them through reliance on God, he learned lessons — lessons that stood him in good stead when he was challenged by this harder, more advanced problem. He had been attending earth's preparatory school, had he not? And what's more, he had been an attentive, receptive, willing, earnest student in this school. He had, through this course of preparation, been growing in his awareness of and absolute trust in God. This proven trust led him to declare: "The Lord that delivered me out of the paw of the lion, and out of the paw of the bear, he will deliver me out of the hand of this Philistine."

Is it any wonder that David declined Saul's offer of armor, explaining, "I have not proved them." With proven, learned trust in God, he ran forward to meet this giant, proclaiming fearlessly that he was facing him "in the name of the Lord of hosts, the God of the armies of Israel." This confidence was a direct result of his spiritual preparation. What a lesson this affords us when we meet our lions and bears, and then our "Goliaths"!

We see similar periods of spiritual training throughout the Bible — in fact, with every one of the Old Testament worthies. Whether it was the tribulation of Job, the preparation and training of Daniel, or of Shadrach, Meshach, and Abednego. The overcoming of a sense of material life as all-in-all was not always a pleasant, easy task; but none of our spiritual predecessors were "drop-outs."

Have you ever stopped to appreciate the fact that the discovery, growth, and continuance of Christian Science has been made possible only through the earnest efforts of thousands upon thousands of willing hearts groping their way through earth's preparatory school? They have cleared the way, often at great human sacrifice, uplifting standards, ennobling human thought out of the Dark Ages through the Renaissance into the Age of Enlightenment — throughout all the centuries preceding our's. Will we do our part in preparing "the way of the Lord"? Our honest efforts should be for the purpose of advancing the kingdom of God upon earth to higher planes of demonstration. And we do this by lifting ourselves to greater spiritual realization.

As in any school the learning process is an individual one. There are some students who may have to repeat a lesson, a course, or even a whole grade. On the other hand, another lesson may be so quickly learned that one moves on to other things almost at once.

If someone does linger over a certain lesson, being unwilling or apparently unable to grasp its principles or meanings, does it benefit another wiser student to go back because of human love and attempt to also repeat the lesson? In an article in the *Christian Science Sentinel* entitled "Borrowed Problems," Louise Knight Wheatley Cook speaks to this question: "There seems to be such a thing as doing too much for people, doing too much for the same ones, smothering them with kindness, doing their growing for them, making their demonstrations for them so that they will be saved the effort.

"We sometimes hear it said, rather sadly: 'My problem is not working out. I have been struggling with it for so long: but try as I may, it does not seem to move.'

"Perhaps the thing which needs to be done in some cases is to see that this problem which never seems to work out was never ours.

"There is this, too, to be remembered. If this thing which has grown to be such a load to us were returned to the one to whom it belongs, it might cease to be a load at all, and become instead only a glorious opportunity wherein the recipient of it finds his wings, and rises to mental heights undreamed of before.

"Let us with gratitude remember that whenever anyone really wishes to enter the kingdom of heaven, he will just walk in of his own accord. The first and most important questions to be considered are these: Does he really desire to enter? Is he really ready to take the necessary steps which he and he alone, must take?

"If he does this not and another one undertakes to carry his burden and do his work, the duty will not be accomplished. No one can save himself without God's help, and God will help each man who performs his own part. After this manner and in no other way is every man cared for and blessed."

We may wonder at times why error appears to us in the particular form and fashion that it does. Why can't we be given another kind of problem, more like the one that Joe has? We could handle that one much more easily!

I think that we have all wondered sometimes why error appears in the particular form that it does. Perhaps the analogy of a leak in a dike might offer helpful insights. Would we ask why the leak appeared when and where it did? We know that water has no intelligence to choose the place or the time of the leak. It simply acts in response to the so-called laws of hydrostatic pressure, seeking the path of least resistance. And when water does flow through a break, it merely reveals a weak spot in the structure which needs strengthening. As we reinforce the dike where the leak occurred, it becomes even stronger than it was before.

Likewise in our human experience, the incessant arguments of material-mindedness seem to be exerting pressure on our mental defenses, constantly testing and probing. When an error or inharmony appears in our experience, it should be treated as a mental leak whose only purpose is to indicate where our spiritual defenses need strengthening.

Often there is a temptation to "probe" mortal thought in an effort to understand why this problem came to us, and why it came at this inconvenient time. Isn't it simply because our defense, our awareness of the falsity of this particular suggestion about life, about the nature of God and His man, was not sufficient? If our defenses were strong enough, the suggestion would never have entered consciousness.

Such mental probing as to the material "why" of error is of no use. In fact, it is counter-productive, and only tends to focus thought on the apparent substance and reality of the erroneous suggestion — on the leak. It starts us out on a psychological witch-hunt, looking for a cause in matter or material circumstance; but there is none. Why not? Because matter is a mental illusion, and there is no cause nor basis to an illusion. All that is important to our growth is that a weakness has been discovered so that our defenses may be strengthened. It is in the repair of the leak, or solving of the problem, that we grow spiritually and find ourselves with a much more impregnable defense. We have learned a lesson in earth's preparatory school.

So when a break, a leak, in our mental defenses, reveals itself, appearing as material discord, a human problem, we use it as a means of learning and strengthening our spiritual defenses. We will then be stronger and more effective for having encountered it — just as the dike is stronger after a weak spot has been discovered and rebuilt.

In school we have little or no choice in the specific problems we are given. Each will serve its own purpose, teach its own lesson. It doesn't matter what the particular problem is, if we simply apply to it the principles that we have diligently endeavored to learn. The application may be done with uncertainty at first; but with growing skill and assurance and practice (application!), we will become more effective students. And we are not tested beyond our ability, training, and understanding. Mrs. Eddy assures us of this in *Science and Health*: "God pours the riches of His love into the understanding and affections, giving us strength according to our day."

As we look back over the preparatory classes of the Scriptural pioneers, our spiritual forefathers, we can see how unique their lessons were. Moses, Jonah, Daniel, Job, Paul, Joseph, Jesus — each one faced learning lessons, it would seem, tailor-made for them. To one it was tending sheep, to one a whale, to another a lions' den, to another physical disease, to Paul it was blindness, to another it was a pit followed by prison, and of course, to our Master it was the cross! Though the particular human experience varied, the purpose of each was to lead him to God.

Now I'd like to speak of a ploy of mortal mind that can easily mislead our efforts and destroy our learning results. How do we assess or grade our schoolwork? How do we determine whether or not we're learning our lessons? What is our standard for measuring success? Can we take outward appearances, material indications of health, riches, worldly success, even human happiness, as a true indication of spiritual accomplishment? Consider this carefully. Aren't material standards used to judge demonstration more often than not? But the irrelevancy of using material standards to judge spiritual accomplishments becomes obvious when we see that many very materially-minded individuals may appear to be more physically robust than their more spiritually-minded counterparts, and even more prosperous. But is this material success, without spiritual growth and understanding, what we seek? Are these material accomplishments what satisfy?

Haven't we all seen instances where people have turned to medical means for healing, and as a result appear to express a sense of health? But clearly, these aren't expressions of God's doing, or of progress Spiritward. Aren't they more like the mathematics student who, rather than working out the problems given in his textbook and so gaining in his understanding of the mathematical principles involved, has turned to the back of the book and copied the answers? Won't he eventually have to repeat the lesson? In *Miscellaneous Writings* our Leader reassures us: "When once you are healed by Science, there is no reason why you should be liable to a return of the disease that you were healed of. But not to be subject again to any disease whatsoever, would require an understanding of the Science by which you were healed."

Now, is there a shortcut, a quick way to attain this sought-after state of spiritual harmony and oneness with God, other than attending earth's preparatory school and truly working out its learning problems? No, I'm sorry to report that neither Abraham, Jacob, Moses, or Daniel — in fact no one, not even our dear Master — ever found a way to evade, avoid, or skip this vitally important schooling. Jonah sure did his best to avoid his assignment, didn't he? But learn it he did, in a damp, dark, rolling classroom he attended on his unscheduled Mediterranean cruise! And tell me, do you think the imperatives of this school are any less demanding or rewarding today than they were for Jonah in his floating classroom some twenty-six centuries ago? The rules remain the same.

But need earth's preparatory school be a grim, joyless experience? No, not unless you are accepting the appearances of the problems as personal realities, and therefore unsolvable. In a schoolroom setting are we discouraged, frustrated, angry, shocked, fearful, or irritated over the problems themselves — fearing they have no solution? Of course not. We may, in fact, find them to be uplifting when we see laws or truths unfolded and illustrated through our efforts to solve them. Even so do we in earth's preparatory school.

So the goal isn't simply to attain physical health, or material wealth, the perfect companion or career (the world's "right answers"); but to gain in spiritual understanding, confidence in Truth, and individual dominion. The "right answers" (the healings) will accompany this understanding as surely as they do in math. But they are only a sign of the deeper things that have been gained through our mental struggles.

It's a case of willingness, isn't it?

We read in Acts where Felix, the Roman procurator, listened to Paul as he preached concerning faith in Christ: "And as he reasoned of righteousness, temperance, and judgment to come, Felix trembled, and answered, Go thy way for this time; when I have a convenient season, I will call for thee."

Are any of us "trembling," but still waiting for a "convenient season" to enroll in earth's preparatory school? I trust it has become clear from the examples of Moses, David, Jonah, and Jesus, that we don't get to vote on whether or not we enroll in earth's preparatory school. It's not a question of *if* we enroll — It is simply a question of *when* we enroll. And what do you think of doing it *now*? Classes are open!

ABOUT THE AUTHOR: Mr. Jensen was a life-long Christian Scientist, and a teacher and practitioner from Richmond, California. He received his Masters degree in Business from the University of Southern California. He attended Hastings College of Law at the University of California and practiced law in Fresno.

He entered the full-time practice of Christian Science in 1964 and became a teacher of Christian Science in 1970. He served as a Field representative for the Mother Church in northern California and also as a Chaplain at San Quentin prison for four years.

Testimony referred to on page 7

The truth that man is spiritual, not material, came to me through my experience in Christian Science. For three or four years I had been an invalid, having several operations. In the last operation it had seemed necessary to remove from my left ear the eardrum and ear bones, and as we are supposed to hear by means of these parts, I was deaf in that ear. In the spring of 1916 I broke down, and the physician who was consulted pronounced my case a tubercular disease. As soon as school closed I went to a sanatorium, hoping to find the health and strength which I needed so much for my work, but instead of getting better, I grew worse all the time. My eyes, which had been weak (glasses having been worn for ten years), gave out rapidly, and I began to fear for my sight. I had stood the strain long, but could not do so any longer, and was on the verge of a nervous breakdown.

I was in this condition when I came to the end of my financial resources and had to go back into the world, though the physician told me that if I should try to work I could not live over six months. When I returned to the city where I lived, a friend offered me the hospitality of her home, but knowing that she was interested in Christian Science I refused. Believing I was sick, I did not want someone to tell me that I was not; for my idea of Christian Science was that its adherents simply thought sickness was imaginary. Still I was not satisfied with the old doctrine which said that God sent sickness and we should pray God to take it away from us. Though I was not willing to acknowledge it, I needed love, and somewhere to rest without worrying, so at last I accepted my friend's invitation, but only after having received her promise that she would not talk about Christian Science to me. The moment I reached her home she had to help me to bed, as I was too feeble to stand and had a burning fever. Before leaving me she handed me the textbook, "Science and Health with Key to the Scriptures" by Mrs. Eddy, telling me to read it if I could not sleep.

How grateful I am for the wisdom which closed her lips and left it to truth to prove itself. Being alone I began to think, and to wonder if Christian Science had wrought the change in her that I had noticed. After a while I came to the conclusion that nothing else could have done it, and having reached this point in my thought I decided that there was some truth in this teaching of which I did not know, and I was going to find out what it was. I forgot my ailments for the moment in my search for this truth, really not giving a thought to the fact that Christian Science was supposed to heal physical troubles.

I opened the textbook and began to read, but my eyes were so weak that I could read only one sentence at a time. Having finished a sentence I would lay the book down and think it over, trying to come to the conclusion as to whether or not I could accept it as true. I would think of what I had read and discuss it from all sides, for I wanted to know the truth but was not willing to accept it simply because others had done so. Every time, however, I came to the conclusion that what I had read was the truth. After having read for twenty minutes I was so filled with the healing thought of this truth, so certain of the presence of a loving Father-Mother God, that there was no room left for any discord.

I got up from the bed and it seemed as if all inharmonious conditions were laid aside as one lays aside a soiled garment. I realized right away that the eyes which a few minutes before had refused to let me read in comfort, were seeing far beyond my human sense of eyesight, and I laid off my glasses at that moment and never used them again. My nerves, which had tried to play havoc with my happiness and reasoning power, heard the command, "Peace, be still," and obeyed. The tubercular trouble with all the rest had gone into the nothingness where it belonged. All this I realized at once, but somehow I did not think of my ears right then, only I knew there was no aching. But that night when trying to find out whether or not my watch had stopped I inadvertently held it to the left instead of the right ear. I had never heard distinctly with my left ear, and how great was my surprise when for the first time in my life, I heard the tick of my watch in that ear, with which I was never supposed to hear again. The eardrum is gone, the hole left by taking out the ear bone is still there, but God does not need these material conditions to make His child perfect. Being a teacher I needed a certificate of health after the doctor had pronounced my case tubercular disease and within two weeks after the experience just related I had two certificates from the best known physicians of the state, saying that I was in perfect health.

This was the beginning of my experience in Christian Science. It is now a year and a half since I found God, and every day has brought a repetition of the blessings realized in those few moments. I am thankful for the physical healing, but the peace and joy which have come into my life, which are there every day, make me so grateful, so happy, that I cannot express it. I am grateful to Mrs. Eddy, who was pure enough to show us the way, to prove to us that Christ Jesus is not merely a beautiful example for us to adore without following, but that what he has done is possible for us to do. I am grateful to know that nothing matters except the knowledge of Truth, the love of God which is reflected in all human beings.

Miss Anna S. Van Leeuwen,
Washington, D.C.
The Christian Science Journal,
March, 1918

For further information regarding Christian Science:
Write: The Bookmark
Post Office Box 801143
Santa Clarita, CA 91380
Call: 1-800-220-7767
Visit our website: www. thebookmark.com